THE UNLIKELY CANDIDATE

THE UNLIKELY CANDIDATE

What Losing an Election Taught Me about How to Change Politics

Ali Milani

First published in Great Britain in 2022 by

Policy Press, an imprint of
Bristol University Press
University of Bristol
1-9 Old Park Hill
Bristol
BS2 8BB
UK
t: +44 (0)117 374 6645
e: bup-info@bristol.ac.uk

Details of international sales and distribution partners are available at
policy.bristoluniversitypress.co.uk

British Library Cataloguing in Publication Data
A catalogue record for this book is available from the British Library

ISBN 978-1-4473-6159-6 paperback
ISBN 978-1-4473-6160-2 ePub
ISBN 978-1-4473-6161-9 ePdf

Cover design: Mark Ecob
Front cover image: Mark Ecob

Bristol University Press and Policy Press use
environmentally responsible print partners.

Printed and bound in Great Britain by TJ Books, Padstow

To Norrette, Andy, James, Jane, Dee, Tim, Ray and all the people (from Uxbridge and South Ruislip and beyond) who believed in us and campaigned alongside us. This is your story as much as it is mine.

To Jaime Marshall and Elisabeth, without whom this book would not have been possible.

To the wonderful team at Policy Press for giving my voice and our story a platform.

And to Haji, Maryam and Maman.

Contents

Foreword

John McDonnell
MP for Hayes and Harlington
Former Shadow Chancellor of the Exchequer

From the outset Ali asks himself how such a young person with only one general election campaign under his belt as a parliamentary candidate can have the front to write a book on his life and experiences.

The answer is that this book needed to be written for all those who want to understand the generation Ali represents, and for all those who need to appreciate the future this generation is to create.

Above all else it needed to be written to inform and inspire members of that generation to press on with its challenge to the debased politics of the present.

Ali is a symbol of that generation of hope, determination and confidence that has emerged in recent years.

In 1997 the Blair government was swept to victory on a wave of joyous enthusiasm. After 13 years of Conservative government people genuinely did believe the line in Labour's campaign song, that 'things can only get better'.

Yet, despite all the early advances in investment in education and health, and the immense breakthrough of the Good Friday Agreement securing peace in Ireland, Blair's Iraq war crushed that spirit of enthusiastic hope.

After 2010 the Conservative and Liberal Democrat coalition government, reneging on promises on tuition fees and imposing a cruel, harsh programme of austerity, risked damaging almost beyond repair any faith young people in particular had in electoral politics.

Instead, it provoked them to take to the streets.

By 2015, after five years of austerity, many young people saw their futures disappearing and even their very existence coming under threat from climate change.

From then onwards a new generation emerged that simply wasn't willing to take it anymore.

Already politically experienced in tuition fees, anti-austerity and environment campaigns, members of this new generation went on to turn back to electoral politics, many of them providing the opening for the election of Jeremy Corbyn as leader of the Labour Party and, more importantly, the advocacy of transformative politics.

Ali Milani embodied this new movement.

This new generation's confidence was built not only on their campaigning experiences, but also on their belief in their potential to bring about transformative change.

This book describes with endearing, fresh-faced and at times heart-rending honesty what many felt and experienced during this remarkable period.

True to form, Ali wears his heart on his sleeve and recounts his and his friends' worries, fears and anxieties as he had the nerve to take on the political battle not just to be a Labour parliamentary candidate, but also to defeat the sitting prime minister in his own constituency.

Ali shares the enthusiasm, the joyous emotional highs for him and his team of activists, of breaking through the barriers that stood in the way of a working-class, Muslim refugee from the Middle East from entering politics in this country.

Importantly, Ali exposes how because of their class and race the system works against young people like him who have that idealistic commitment to simply want to play a role in public life.

This book is a valuable riposte to any who doubt the scale of Islamophobia faced by young Muslims, who dare to put their heads above the political parapet in this country. It is a challenge to the Labour Party to face up to recognising and addressing Islamophobia within the party itself.

In its treatment of Ali's election campaign, the role of the British media is displayed in all its glory, from the good and the bad to the downright ugly, and at times, farcical.

The shadowy, corrupt financing of our political system is depicted alongside the financial hardship faced by a working-class young person trying to break into our political structures.

Ali also sets out not just a critique of how the Labour Party and other political parties throw up bureaucratic and political barriers preventing them from truly reflecting the diversity of our community, but also a series of reforms that could help tear down those barriers.

Although Ali fought an intensive, creative and inspirational election campaign, the mountain to climb in the political moment of 2019 was insurmountable.

Since then, with a change in leader, the Labour Party and electoral politics have entered a different political space that has, for many, deterred them from party politics.

Although we may have moved on from those initial days of hope when Ali Milani had, what some thought, was the audacity to stand as a Labour candidate to oust the prime minister, just like him, young people have politically not gone away.

They have become the marchers in Black Lives Matter, Extinction Rebellion, the Women's movement, active in campaigns to support asylum-seekers, renters unions and on trade union picket lines across the country in a wave of new unionism.

They are deploying all the campaigning techniques and new technology that many of them harnessed and refined in Ali's selection and election campaign.

They are the sleeping giant of politics in this country with the immense potential to combine again the politics of the street and picket line with the politics of the ballot box.

This story of a young, working-class Muslim taking on the heights of the political establishment will serve as an inspirational handbook.

Introduction: 'Hope'

Hope in politics today is in serious short supply.

Wherever I looked, I saw a generation despondent and disconnected. Young people walking across cities and states in the United States demanding common-sense reform to end the cycle of gun violence they were facing in their schools. A single teenage girl standing outside the Swedish Parliament crying out to the world to tackle the existential threat of climate change. A young man at the beginning of his adult life languishing in an Egyptian prison, for having the audacity to believe in a different future.

Both in the UK and all across the world, a whole generation of us found ourselves politically detached. Just as we were reaching the defining moments of our time, with crises after crises demanding international cooperation and organisation, we were seeing all the wrong men, in all the wrong places, at all the wrong times. As the Amazon rainforest burned, as COVID-19 gripped the world, and as our oceans rose, it wasn't our generation leading the fight. It was Boris Johnson, and Donald Trump, and Jair Bolsonaro, and Abdel Fattah al-Sisi, and Narendra Modi, and an entire global political establishment either unable or unwilling to meet the true scale of the challenges that lay ahead.

Yet despite all of this, I believe I have found hope. A reason to believe.

★ ★ ★

As my father and I sit on a small balcony in the heart of Istanbul, the rays of sun cut across the small table that separated us, almost as if to highlight our two worlds. After nearly three years of distance and in the middle of a volatile political campaign, my father and I had found time to reconnect. We had spent most of our lives apart – he was living in Tehran, unable to come to the UK, and I in London, unable to return to return to Iran.

1

It was October 2019 and my world had changed, probably forever. As we approached what we anticipated to be the final months of our campaign, I had been sent away – through the insistence of my team – for one final break before the final round of this political fight.

We had rented a one-bed apartment for the week, up a small alleyway, just a minute's walk from the heart of Istanbul. So, as we sat with a cup of tea in front of us, squeezed in by the metal perimeter of the balcony, we could just about hear the hum of the city. It seemed poetic to me – we were probably just a few months away from election day in the UK, and while I was sitting embracing the peaceful sunlight, the distant hum was a reminder of what awaited me back in London.

I had a sense of just how much life had changed on my journey – from the pats on the back I received from security staff at Heathrow, to being removed from the 'randomly selected' extra baggage check as the supervisor recognised my name. But nothing had brought me back down to earth like sharing a cup of tea with my old man.

As afternoon turned to evening, and evening into night, I told him the whole story. The long, rollercoaster journey of the previous 13 months – with every twist, every turn and every challenge. My dad sat back and listened, occasionally interjecting to ask about how things worked in the UK. For us, this was normal. Much of the (limited) time we had spent together while I was growing up was often on balconies or over cups of teas discussing politics, philosophy, poetry and more. He in his youth had witnessed revolutions and regime changes, and I, in mine, was fascinated by them. Our discussions often lasted long enough whereby we might have missed day turning into night, and night turning into day.

Unbeknownst to me, there was something different about this particular discussion. As I sat telling the tale of the last year of my life, my dad had noticed something different about me. He would describe it as a flicker of light. He had seen in my face a new and infectious element: hope. In my teenage years, he would often tease me with a saying: 'My generation went out and overthrew a king, what are you going to do?' As I finished telling my story that afternoon, he said to me that I had finally found what I was going to do.

That was one of the last in-person conversations we would ever have, as my trip to Istanbul would be the last time I would see him before we lost him to COVID-19 in March 2020. But the idea for this book came about just before his passing. I didn't want to do it at first. It seemed ludicrous for a 20-something-year-old to write a book about their 'life' story.

'Tell what story? It's still happening!' I would often say. But my dad had a different belief. He wanted me to tell the same story I had told him that afternoon. From that warm balcony, sat right on the border between East and West, I had shown him that I had come to believe in hope once again. That belief and hope could now be translated into practice. And so that is what this book is. Not a political memoir or a manifesto, but just my story and my reflections – so that your face may be filled with just some of the same hope mine was that day, the hope I hold on to this very day. So that down the road we may fight for a better world together.

1

'A great idea, but probably not for someone like me'

I must have found a million excuses not to do it. I was too young. Too inexperienced. No one would take me seriously.

It is a fact that is as old as politics itself: the best leaders are often those who are the most reluctant to lead. Those who look on from a distance, knowing they have so much to contribute, yet can't bring themselves to believe they are qualified, electable or even worthy. Although I wouldn't belong in the company of those great leaders, the image of someone unworthy and under-qualified is certainly one that I had crafted for myself. I believed that this world of politics was not for 'someone like me'.

When I thought the idea through, it made perfect sense. Ali Milani standing as the Labour Party candidate against Boris Johnson in my home seat of Uxbridge and South Ruislip made sense. As just an idea. For years I had been arguing in our community and within our local party that we needed to diversify our political figures. I had walked into far too many meetings with mostly retired, white faces, who were incredibly kind and passionate, who gave up their time and energy to fight for the most vulnerable in our society; but who – ultimately – would themselves readily accept that they did not fully represent the multiformity of Uxbridge and South Ruislip constituency.

We needed more young people, we needed more black and brown faces, and we certainly needed more leaders who came 'from within'. So as an idea, it made all the sense in the world. But to go from an idea to a plan, and a plan to a campaign, was a wholly different proposition. In my heart, I knew that this particular campaign story would be poetic, that my mere presence on the stage, as a young, working-class immigrant, could ignite so much belief. If we got it right and told our story, it could be the single most powerful election campaign in the whole country (knowing who our opponent would be). In fact, if I were advising someone else in a different, far-away constituency facing the same decision, I would be telling them that they *had* to do it. The very unlikeliness of the story and candidacy was its real strength. It was too important a moment for the party and the country not to. The task of making the unlikely happen was, after all, what great movements and campaigns were all about.

But I could not allow myself to be a character in this particular story. It *was* a great idea, I admitted, but probably not for 'someone like me'.

I have come to realise over the years that the greatest political barriers our communities face are often not the ones that are physically erected in front of us; they are the ones that are slowly implanted into our mind through the course of our lives. The images of politicians dressed in tailor-made suits, drinking brandy, surrounded by grandeur and luxury. The Etonian, Oxbridge graduates who have doors opened before them as they arrive into every room, and their futures guaranteed from infancy. The Boris Johnsons and David Camerons of this world, who, with all their privilege and money, are seemingly chiselled from birth and placed on a conveyor belt to public office. These simple images and ideas that are conditioned into most of us from youth fester into a very simple notion: political office is a birthright for the rich and powerful, and not something for 'the likes of us'.

In the earliest parts of my journey, it was this mountain built in my subconscious that I found the hardest to climb – to remind myself that the best public servants most often come from within the communities they aim to serve. They are those people who don't speak of the struggles and hardships of their constituents as an abstract concept, but through their own lived experiences. They are, in short, those who understand what it's like to 'live like us'. The toughest part of this extraordinary and unlikely campaign we embarked on was not the mechanics of campaigning, or the scrutiny of mainstream media, or the financial pressures, or even the global attention that came with taking on a sitting prime minister; it was first convincing myself I could do it, to unlearn the conditioning of what a politician 'looked' and 'sounded' like. It was convincing myself that I was old enough, experienced enough, and worthy.

★ ★ ★

When my phone rang, I didn't recognise the number. Most of the people I have known in my life rarely pick up an unrecognised or blocked number, but for some reason, my curiosity has never allowed me to let a call go unanswered – a ringing phone should always be answered. This particular phone call, taking place on a cold, wet afternoon in central London, would change my life forever.

At the time I got the call I was in the middle of a training seminar at the Institute of Education (IOE), which sits in the heart of London, sandwiched between Russell Square and Euston Station. An uninspiring tower block, a stone's throw away from SOAS University and the British Museum, you would be forgiven for having never noticed it on your wanders towards its neighbours. While thousands of tourists, commuters and locals walk past its bullish figure every day, I doubt many have ever glanced at it twice.

Despite its external face not baring anything particularly inspiring or noteworthy, inside it is usually bustling with energy and pace. Predominately a space for lectures, seminars and the occasional conference, on a busy day it can feel like walking through a market or a bazaar. Students walking with singular purpose, headphones on, with no care or expectation from the outside world. Teachers racing between classes, occasionally stopping to point people in the right direction. And then there are those like me.

IOE has one very special thing about it that no other university or college building in the local area has: they *never* lock their classroom doors. You could walk through on a busy Wednesday afternoon or an empty Saturday morning – the teaching rooms will always be open.

And for this reason alone, the IOE has been home to student political organising for as long as I can remember. If we needed a meeting to organise a student protest? We went to the IOE. If we needed a space for a training session or to deliver a political briefing? We went to the IOE. If we needed a space to write speeches, make banners or even send out press releases for one of our carefully plotted plans? We went to the IOE. It is therefore incumbent upon me, at this time, to send my deepest and most sincere thanks to the Institute of Education for many years of (unknown) service to student political organising.

I can recall days where we would stay late into the night, or on weekends where there were clearly no conferences or classes; we would have a familiar dance with the one security officer who seemed to do the job alone. As this older Caribbean man strolled through the corridors, he would knock on our door and ask if we had booked the room we were using. We never did, although we would always insist with absolute certainty that we had. He would then ask to see a reservation, and I would look down at my phone in frantic search of an email that both of us knew we didn't have. Our game of chicken would commence. Did he care enough to stand in limbo in the corridor waiting to see our reservation? Would I be brazen enough to keep pretending to search on my phone for an email that we both knew didn't exist? Through a combination of our tenacity – but mostly his not caring enough to stand around for 20 minutes – we almost always won. He would (kindly) move on to the next room, and we would reconvene our congress of organising.

By early January 2018 I had been serving as Vice-President (Union Development) (VP UD) of the National Union of Students (NUS UK) for a few months. Having spent two years as President of Brunel University's Students' Union, I had been elected to take up the position of VP UD in the NUS at the annual conference in Brighton the preceding spring. As the first Muslim to be elected into this position, and following a conference where my side of the political aisle had lost every election except mine, I was committed to rebuilding our electoral chances in time for the next conference one year on.

The NUS UK is the biggest and best-funded student organisation anywhere on the planet. With over 500 affiliated student unions, spanning across universities and colleges all over the country, it has historically been one of the key institutional actors in British politics. In my time in the organisation, it had over 20 full-time officers representing more than 7 million members.

I always felt the weight of being 'the first Muslim' the heaviest of all the responsibilities I had had. I was astutely aware that as a Muslim, my actions and decisions would be projected onto all other Muslim activists and officers around the country, whether they shared my political views or not. I knew that I would be subject to disproportionate accountability, the sharp end of the right-wing press and the vitriol of a governing Conservative Party that had no problem turning its fire on me and the NUS as a consequence. It was the first time in my life I felt the loneliness and weight that comes with the responsibility of 'elected office'.

So I often focused my attention on ensuring we had a wave of young new activists getting involved in student activism and politics. When it came to student politics, I was, and am to this day, a romantic. I believed that through sheer force of numbers, we could accomplish the goals we had set for ourselves. We could train, develop and support thousands of bright minds and determined young people on university and college campuses all over the country. This, in my view, would give young people and students a fighting chance against a government that had delivered blow after blow to our generation for nearly a decade.

On this cold January afternoon, we used one of the 'free rooms' provided to us by the wonderful people in the IOE to host a training seminar with the Federation of Student Islamic Societies (FOSIS). FOSIS, at this time, shared my view that it was important to give young Muslim students the knowledge and tools to make a difference in their individual campuses. I delivered a presentation highlighting how the NUS worked and the different ways they could each get involved. I pointed to the history of the student movement – from fighting South African Apartheid to keeping Britain out of the Vietnam War – as evidence of the power students could hold if harnessed correctly. The presentation was met with an all too familiar reaction I had become used to as Vice-President of the NUS – mostly indifference, a lot of scepticism, and a hint of interest scattered across the room.

At the conclusion of my session I retreated to the back of the room, as I often did at these events, to observe the rest of the seminar as a casual observer. My phone rang. Not recognising the number and not wanting to disturb the seminar, I stepped outside into the grey abandoned corridor to answer.

'Hello ... is that Ali Milani?'

'Hi, yes, sorry I don't have this number saved. ... Who's this?'

'It's Rosie [not her real name] ... from Momentum.'

'Ah, of course, Rosie! Long time, how have you been?' [I had *no idea* who Rosie was.]

'I'm okay thanks. I was just calling as the parliamentary selections in Uxbridge are due to start and we were wondering if you might be interested in standing?'

In my admittedly brief career in electoral politics, I had encountered a number of tactics to convince candidates to run. I had even employed a few of them myself. There is flattery: 'No one can do this job better than you.' Then there is urgency: 'We need you now more than ever.' There is even guilt: 'Without you, we have no chance.' But Rosie had opted for quite a different approach, one I was unfamiliar with and have since come to define as 'blunt force trauma'. Just like that, within three sentences, she had implanted an idea into my mind that would change my entire future.

I stopped for a moment to process the question. At first, I was sure I had misheard. Perhaps Rosie was looking for recommendations for someone to stand? Or maybe she was talking about a local council election or local constituency party position? When she clarified that she was indeed talking about me standing to be an MP, the full scale of the question hit me: I was being asked to stand to be the Labour Party's parliamentary candidate against Boris Johnson.

'No thanks.'

I quickly hung up the phone.

★ ★ ★

When I was first drawn into political activism, the idea that I might eventually be standing for public office never entered my wildest imagination. Growing up in my community, trust in politics was not in great supply. We had developed, over time and through our own individual experiences, an angst and anger at the world that had been built around us. While in our early youth we may not have been able to eloquently articulate it, deep in the pits of our stomachs we knew that there was something seriously wrong. The poverty on our estates, the countless friends we lost to crime and the desert of opportunities that seemed to lie before us. All of this contributed to our hopelessness in politics and our lack of faith in politicians. To us, they were all the same.

My family and I came to the UK as asylum-seekers from Iran. We arrived in London when I was just five years old, not speaking a word of English, and with almost no money to our name. My mother risked her life and all her possible futures to cross continents on a simple promise: that here, her children would be looked after when they were sick, educated when they were young, and given opportunities to be whoever they may want to be. In many ways, this promise was fulfilled. When we fell sick, we were cared for by a National Health Service that never asked us to reach into our pockets. Our local schools and teachers accepted us as one of their own in an instant, and without hesitation or suspicion. We were given shelter by a local council when we had no place to call home and no friends to rely on. On this island, thousands of miles from the land where we were all born, we would build a home and a new life.

And we were not alone. Living on a council estate as an immigrant family with a single parent was no unique story in North West London. We were surrounded by a community whose stories closely resembled our own. Walking through our estate, you would see faces and cultures that reflected the true tapestry of what I would come to know about modern Britain. From the immigrant family upstairs to the white British couple next door, we all lived similar lives and had the same day-to-day struggles and challenges. There was a beautiful and painful solidarity to it all. If we had a difficult month and only ate one meal in the day, or skipped breakfast before school because mum had had her benefits cut off, we did not think too much of it, as it was a familiar story among our friends and classmates. For most of my early life, I thought this world was the only world that existed in Britain.

But as I grew up and age cleared the fog of childhood, I began seeing a different picture. I watched the politicians and our country's leaders on TV, and I saw faces and lives that neither reflected me nor the lives of anyone I knew. I slowly began seeing the growing inequality and the scale of poverty across our community. Most significantly, I began to feel the pain. As my youthful ignorance began to lift, I felt the pain of all of our parents struggling to put food on the table. I felt the sorrow of losing my friends to a knife. And I felt anger – anger about not just the inequality and injustice within our society, but also the missed opportunities. We were being held back and I knew something had to change. I had felt first hand the generosity, the openness and kind spirit of this community. I could not yet articulate it, but I knew then, in my heart, what Britain could be; we just had to have the courage to fight for it. Our struggle in those days was a collective effort just to be heard. Politicians seemed a distant and detached breed. We watched them in Parliament, grunting and shouting in their ritualised way on those familiar green benches, but we never saw ourselves in them. I always imagined that my contribution to politics would be from the outside shouting in, demanding justice for those like me. I can remember distinctly when my shouting began. I can remember the moment I became conscious of the political anger that would fuel my journey into politics.

The election result of 2010 had given the UK a hung Parliament. Nick Clegg, who had impressed many in the election campaign, agreed to work with Conservative Party leader David Cameron and to form the first coalition government since the Second World War. In the first year of this new coalition government, Cameron and Clegg decided to lift the cap on university tuition fees from £3,000 to £9,000, trebling the cost of higher education for millions of students.

My cohort was the first to pay this price. A generation of politicians, who had all received their education for free, were now telling us that we had to accrue over £50,000 worth of debt to get an education. They had the power, in a single afternoon, to change our entire future, and there seemed to be nothing we could do. The palpable anger in our classroom the day the policy was announced is burned into my mind. None of us had ever held much hope for politicians before this, but for the very first time, most of us felt directly cheated by them. We felt the sting of Westminster. I can recall vividly, as if it were yesterday, a conversation with our philosophy and ethics teacher that afternoon. Michael Parker – an older teacher who was identifiable from any distance by his snow-white hair – faced a barrage of questions: 'How can they do this?', 'How can they get away with it?', 'What can we do to stop it?'

Mr Parker, fielding questions like a press secretary in a news conference, answered in a way that would transform my worldview. He spoke pure truth: 'Because you can't vote, and because they think there is nothing you will do about it.' I hear a lot of people talk about defining moments in their lives, a moment in time that changed their future forever. If I had one in my life, this is it. Congregating around a small wooden table in our college common room, we knew we had to do something. The challenge had been laid out and we were determined to meet it. In a single moment, our angst, anger and disappointment was given an outlet.

A glassed-in room on the ground floor of our newly refurbished school building, the college common room was sacred ground. Reserved only for sixth form students, for years we had looked on with keen anticipation for the day we would be allowed to go inside and use it. With university prospectuses on the bookshelves providing an ironic backdrop, this room was now home to our revolution. Plotting around that small wooden table, we came to a unanimous agreement on how we could fight back. We planned to organise a mass walk-out on 24 November 2010 to join the country-wide student protests in Westminster.

November 24 was a bitterly cold Wednesday afternoon. Having spent weeks organising, printing leaflets and talking with every class, we had successfully mobilised almost the entirety of our cohort to join the walk-out and demonstration. Teachers and school administrators had tried to deter students by threatening cuts to our Educational Maintenance Allowance (a £30 weekly payment some students would receive), detentions, or even possible exclusions as ways to stop us protesting – but all efforts proved futile. Nearly a hundred students packed into the common room that day waiting for their signal to walk across the school grounds and to take back our future.

The 2010 student demonstrations in London have since become a significant moment for British politics. Pictures of the Millbank occupation and the 'kettling' of students on London Bridge are immediately recognisable for anyone from that generation. The discernible anger and energy that radiated from those crowds into every classroom and common room was felt for months after. For those of us demonstrating it was also a significant political psychological moment. It opened our eyes to the reality of where power lies in our country. It created a new generation of political activists.

I took the bus back from London Bridge that Wednesday afternoon, believing we had won. Euphoric on the journey home, I walked through my front door, believing I had played a part in making history and re-orientating the future of my classmates and my generation. But in the weeks that followed the demonstration, it became apparent that the government had no intention of listening to the cries of tens of thousands of students and young people. That for all our organising and mobilising, for all our efforts to engage and our insistence to be heard, we would be met with silence.

On 9 December 2010, following our demonstrations and protests, Parliament voted 323 to 302 to increase the cap on tuition fees and to burden my generation with huge amounts of debt.[1] This vote passed critically with the support of many Liberal Democrats, who had, in the previous election, campaigned explicitly not to increase tuition fees. Over the weeks and months that followed this decision, I became despondent. As the government passed these new educational reforms into law, I became conscious of my own powerlessness and distance between our actions and our future. Sure, we had never really believed in mainstream politics anyway, but once I had seen the thousands of young people take to the streets of London, I was convinced we would be listened to. That somehow things would change. I naively believed that no government could ignore the wave of anger and action that students had just displayed across the country. I was wrong.

The gap that exists between our young people and mainstream electoral politics is no accident. It is entirely by design and functioning as intended. It is the combination of a structural, institutional design created to lock out unwanted ideas and people, and a culture of exclusion and inaccessibility that discourages the most talented among young, minority and working-class communities from participating. All of this is built with the singular purpose of creating a conveyor belt of politicians who all look, speak and act within a predetermined paradigm of acceptable discourse. This ensures that no matter the outcome of any single election or popular trend, the interests of the wealthiest and most privileged in our society are never at risk.

There is no better way to display this elitist political system than to point to those who have sat atop the throne of our parliamentary democracy. In modern British democracy history, 22 of our prime ministers have been educated at Eton College, 7 at Harrow School and 6 at Westminster School. These three most elite and exclusive educational institutions account for a staggering 35 prime ministers dating all the way back to the 1800s. As we look to see if similar trends exist within higher education, we find that it only gets worse. The Universities of Cambridge and Oxford, two of the most elite educational institutions on the planet (and commonly referred to as 'Oxbridge'), account for a staggering 42 prime ministers, the closest other institutions being the Universities of Glasgow and Edinburgh, both of which educated three prime ministers.

Neither is this just confined to Number 10. As of spring 2019, a Sutton Trust study found that 39 per cent of the government's Cabinet and 29 per cent of all Members of Parliament (MPs) had been educated in a private independent school, compared to 7 per cent of the population. During the same period, Oxford and Cambridge had educated 21 per cent of all MPs, while a further 33 per cent had attended another 'Russell Group' university.[2] This snapshot view of Britain's corridors of power tells us something we all already know: that our politics better resembles the tea rooms of private schools than the common rooms most of us grew up in.

Many often argue that this is simply the result of a 'better quality of education' that private schools provide, largely due to better class sizes, teaching and resources. And in some areas, they would be right. But we also know that this isn't all that private schools provide. They are also institutions of social reproduction, of nurturing and networking for a cohort of often wealthy students (with often wealthy parents), pointing them directly to the most powerful institutions and offices. These statistics and this culture are also not something that exist outside the public consciousness. Quite the contrary, it is an accepted norm within common political understandings. In my school and college, it was unchallenged and accepted that those who occupy the highest office of public service must come from schools such as Eton or Harrow or Westminster. And those schools were certainly not usually places for an immigrant child who had grown up on a council estate with a single mother on benefits. I knew all of this to be true, and so, despite a burning passion to roll up my sleeves and participate in mainstream politics, I accepted that this road would never be for me.

I found myself going through a real transformation over the spring of 2011. The failure of our demonstrations to achieve any meaningful change in government policy had a deep effect on me. The voice of my generation was clearly irrelevant to those at the very top of our politics. Determined to never again feel that powerless, I became devoted to changing the way our politics worked. I had felt in the bluntest way the distance between Westminster and my generation, between politicians and my community – and I was committed to bridging that gap. My despondence very quickly morphed into drive. One thing that had become clear at this time was that our decision-makers were not just unwilling to represent us, but were also, in many ways, *incapable*. They had never lived a day in our shoes. They had no idea what our world was like and what our lives were like. That realisation, and my dawning belief that political representation has to spring from some degree of identification, from empathy, and simply from knowledge of what life is like for most people, is what drove me to run for office and what fuels my political activity. Our communities deserve leaders who know what it is like to 'live like us', who have felt the pain of poverty, the trauma of losing friends to crime, the despair, the hopelessness. In a healthy democracy, no one should feel powerless.

There has always seemed to me to be some rather simple changes we could make to radically change our attitudes towards engaging young people in politics in the UK. The lowering of the voting age to 16 is an obvious first step any government could make to show its commitment to young voters. It escapes me to this day how 16- and 17-year-olds can go to work and pay their taxes, yet have no say in how those taxes are spent. This, in essence 'taxation without representation', in my mind, is not only a principal democratic deficit that exists within our country, but also a moral deficit. Opponents to the call for votes at 16 have long claimed that young people are simply not mature enough to be custodians of something as important as a ballot. That their immaturity would have profound impacts on the direction of the country. Yet (conveniently) they often ignore that our existing law deems 16- and 17-year-olds mature and competent enough to give full medical consent, to enter into a civil partnership or marriage, to become the director of a company and to join the armed forces. It is safe to say that those who oppose the extension of voting rights to 16-year-olds have only one thing to fear: the way young people *would* vote.

In 2015, former Prime Minister David Cameron agreed to allow the Scottish Parliament the power to reduce the voting age for the upcoming Scottish independence referendum. Knowing the campaign to keep Scotland in the UK would need the support of young people, he allowed the voting age to be reduced without worrying about the maturity of these young voters. And they did not disappoint. The referendum saw 80 per cent of eligible 16- to 17-year-olds register to vote and a 75 per cent turnout among this registered group.[3] It became clear that one part of the criticisms for lowering the voting age was certainly true: young people *could* have profound impacts on the direction of our country.

Further to the extension of the voting age, we can simply embed our parliamentary democracy into the foundations of our education system and in the culture of growing up in the UK. I have always found it rather strange that in every election and every referendum, we shut down schools to provide space for local constituents to vote, yet we make no effort to engage the young minds that occupy these schools on a daily basis, to give them the opportunity to participate in that electoral process. Most are sent home for the day and expected to return once the voting and counting has been completed, and none come out of the process any the wiser of democracy or electoral politics. What is stopping us from integrating the students of that school into the running of these elections? What if, rather than simply being sent home for the day, they were made fundamental to the process and given a live education on the importance and value of engagement in our democracy? This would surely not only break down conscious and unconscious barriers that exist between young people and the ballot box, but would also integrate democracy into their educational experience.

The UK already falls desperately behind other comparable countries in our levels of youth engagement in mainstream politics and turnout. The 2019 General Election saw 47 per cent turnout among 18- to 24-year-olds compared to 68 per cent in the 2017 German federal elections and 66 per cent in the Netherlands 2017 general election.[4] Contrary to right-wing talking points, this is not because of intrinsic political apathy among young people in Britain. Even a cursory view of our political discourse over the past 10 years shows clearly how young people have influenced the political debate. From race, to gender, to sexual orientation, most of the progress being made in progressive political debate is being driven by a new generation of engaged citizens. Yet this isn't translating into voting turnout.

Why? Because my experience of disappointment, despondence and disillusionment following the student protests of 2010 is far too universal and familiar. For all of our lives, young voters have not seen themselves or their worldview represented within mainstream politicians or political parties. Issues such as racial equality, climate change, the levels of violence in our communities, a free and transformative education system and an ethical foreign policy have had to make way for neoliberal economics and wars. We have been persistently told to settle, to pick the lesser of two evils and to grow up when we have demanded fundamental change. The student protestors of 2010 were told to settle for a graduate tax, the young #BlackLivesMatter activists told to accept incremental training changes to policing, and those who are fighting ferociously for the future of our planet forced to wait until 2050 for any serious action. All of this is enough to disassociate any voter base from participating, but combined with a conscious and tactical unwillingness to embed political education into our national curriculum, this often leaves young people as passengers in our democracy – living with the consequences, but with little involvement with the direction.

But if the last decade has shown us anything, it is that we can no longer afford to be sat on the sidelines. Just in the years following that cold, dark night on London Bridge in 2010, my generation has had to endure the trebling of tuition fees, the eradication of maintenance grants, an era of austerity, massive wage stagnation not seen since the Napoleonic wars, Brexit, and the shambolic mishandling of a global pandemic. There seems to be a growing consciousness of the fact that we can no longer expect change to take place with people who are simply incapable of understanding the experiences of people around the country. Too much is at stake now, from the lives of our loved ones to the future of our planet. The gap between the young and the Houses of Parliament must now be closed – as a matter of urgency – and that can only be achieved through the committed effort of both the dismantling of institutional barriers and the changing of our political culture, a collective effort for young people to engage and to lead.

Maybe I shouldn't have ended Rosie's phone call so abruptly.

★ ★ ★

For weeks following that phone call, the idea of standing in my home seat of Uxbridge and South Ruislip circled round my head. It bounced between the ludicrous and the obvious. I went from being sure I could do it, to laughing away any prospect that I could ever be taken seriously. Perhaps if I had gone to a school with a long lineage of political leaders, or had walked through the corridors of Eton, or Harrow, or Westminster, I could have somehow absorbed the natural confidence and inclination to thrust myself into the election. Yet, despite having competed in and won both national elections in the UK and a local election in Hillingdon, I feared the embarrassment of being laughed out of the room by my own local party. Still, over time, the proposition took up enough space and capacity in my thinking that I decided to consult some trusted confidants. I thought it best to present the idea to people I believed would be honest enough with me so that, if the idea was as ludicrous as parts of my own mind believed it to be, they would tell me without worry of hurting my feelings. I needed some blunt force.

If there was anywhere I could find that, it was within a trusted circle I had built for myself. Over my many elections at the NUS and local government, I had found myself often retreating to a group of trusted friends and confidants who, at least in the world of student politics, had always stood by me and proven themselves highly capable and competent. As the media often hounded us and the pressures of student politics reached a tipping point, a group of friends who would give honest and non-judgmental advice was invaluable. First among them was Yusuf Hassan. Yusuf, himself a second-generation Somali immigrant from East London, was then Vice-President of FOSIS, and a close friend throughout my journey in student politics.

When I presented him with the idea of standing for Parliament against Boris Johnson in Uxbridge, he seemed lukewarm to the idea. He quickly expressed his reservations that after our recent re-election campaign in the NUS and close-fought local election campaign in Hillingdon, another high-profile election race may be one too many. He also questioned whether a constituency Labour Party (CLP) that was largely older and white might not naturally look for a 'safer' candidate in such a high-profile race. He was right.

It was entirely possible that even if members of our local party liked me and believed I might do a good job, the nature of the task might incline them towards a more traditional, safer choice. Ultimately, I took two key things from our conversation: (1) Yusuf's reservations were probably right – the chances of us winning were quite slim, but (2) he didn't think the idea was ludicrous. He didn't laugh me out of the room or say that I should have my head examined (as he had for plenty of other ideas I had presented him with over the years). The part of my mind that thought this whole thing was a fantasy began to shrink for the first time.

I had gotten into a strange habit, since my days as the Students' Union President at Brunel, to write anecdotal and often random speeches on the notes section of my phone as ideas sprung to mind. I might hear a word or a phrase that I found powerful, and I would find myself writing a speech on the bus home, centred round this single word or phrase. Fascinated by speechwriting and speeches as a form of political power and persuasion, it became a fun pastime for me on my long travels while at the NUS. Sometimes my notes would come in handy for an impromptu speech at a conference or members event, but most of them would never see the light of day. For a few months following my tussle with the idea of standing for Parliament, I would write speeches that told the story of what I imagined *Ali Milani vs Boris Johnson* to be. Sat on a cold 467 bus from Shepherd's Bush back to Uxbridge, I would exuberantly type on my iPhone's miniature keypad the ultimate David and Goliath political story. It wasn't just about a single election, or even a competition between two political parties; it was a question of who we were as a country. Did Britain have within it the capacity to let someone like me, with my upbringing and disadvantages, with all my faults and imperfections, to take on and even defeat a former Mayor of London and the most recognisable face in British politics? Could a working-class, local resident unseat the face of the British political establishment? Imagine the implications. This could change everything.

These little notes and rants sketched on cold buses and crammed underground journeys were beginning to convince even me. Not just because of the power of the story, but because I believed in the country and the community that I was writing about. I believed it was within our and my capacity to make this story a reality. As I began to come around to the idea, I decided to pitch it to the entirety of my confidant group, and to see what the general consensus might be. Late into a spring evening, as all nine of us were crammed into my small studio apartment in Uxbridge, I presented the idea as it had been pitched to me by Rosie. I painted the picture of what I thought the campaign could be, and the power behind the story that might inspire a unique campaign. I looked around for a response. My studio being no bigger than 35 × 35 feet and consisting of one single room, with a bed on one side, a desk to work from on the other and an open kitchen squeezed into the far corner, it was hard for anyone to hide their instinctual responses – some were sat on the desk, a couple on the bed and the rest of us squeezed together on the floor.

Yusuf spoke first, having had a head start on the idea, and raised the same reasonable reservations he had had before. He was concerned about fatigue, the publicity of the election, and whether there was any chance I would even be considered in the primary election. The others in the room seemed to share his general sentiment and reluctance. As others chimed in, I began to sense a general theme to the concerns being raised – most were worried that even just running in the primary election may hurt my standing within the NUS (where I still had a term to serve), and some feared running for Parliament at such a young age would get me branded with the dreaded 'career politician' tag. The latter point never really concerned me – I was as far away from a career politician as it could get – I wasn't aware of any other 'career politician' in Westminster having been born in Tehran and raised on benefits by a single mother on a council estate.

The first voice in the room to openly support the idea of me running was Sayed Al Kadiri. Sayed had been my campaign manager for both my NUS national elections and knew (better than anyone perhaps) what I would be like as a candidate. A man of Yemeni origin, Sayed had gained the reputation as the old man of our group, as, even at the age of 29, his mannerisms and behaviour better resembled someone in their later years. In his usual calm and subdued way, he leaned back on my bed and made the case that this was a unique opportunity: 'When else is Ali going to get an opportunity to go up against someone like Boris Johnson?' Abdi-Aziz, nicknamed 'the Professor', and our Northern representative from Yorkshire, agreed. As the philosophy graduate and deep thinker of the team, he often thought in bigger terms than the rest of us. His thought was: even if we did not win, there were advantages to putting my name in the hat and seeing what happened – the possibilities of defining the debate, of raising the issues of racism, of inequality, making sure an eventual candidate understood the backdrop this election would take place under. After an evening of long debate, at around 3am I asked everyone to vote on two questions: (1) Did they think I should stand in the primary election? (2) Did they think I had any chance of winning? On both questions it was an overwhelming 'no'. To my recollection only three out of nine thought I should even stand, and a confidence-building zero out of nine thought I could win. There was one, crucial, caveat. Everyone believed that as no one (other than me) present was a local resident and knew the politics of our local area well, I should probably gather the views of local CLP members. If they were excited by the prospect of someone like me running and were prepared to get on board, then I would have to consider it.

'Pick five local people you trust, ask them honestly, and if they say "yes", or even "maybe", then we can have start to have a conversation about throwing your name in the hat.'

★ ★ ★

Alone and in a secluded cafe opposite Uxbridge Station, I began to write a list of names, top of which was John McDonnell.

John had been the MP for Hayes and Harlington since 1997, the neighbouring constituency to ours in Uxbridge and South Ruislip. Short in stature with striking white hair and contrasting black eyebrows, he had a reputation for being a fighter on the left of the Labour Party. One edition of the *Spectator* in 2018 described him as the 'hard man of the left' with an accompanied front page caricature of him wielding knuckle dusters ready for a fight.[5] Those who knew John would never have recognised these pictures or caricatures. They would know a kind and committed public servant who has only every fought for those in desperate need. Growing up in Liverpool as a child to a docker and a cleaner, John had seen and felt the pain of poverty within working-class communities, and developed an insatiable appetite for building a fairer, more equal society. As a public orator and media performer, he is one of the most skilled in the UK, and has a particular talent among the left of capturing the anger and passion that comes from within these communities – probably largely because he continues to be one of them to this day.

I first met John in the late spring of 2013. As a first year student of International Politics at Brunel University (also his alma mater), I had signed up to attend a seminar he was hosting alongside our Politics and Labour Society. At the time, I didn't know anything about him. To me he was an unnamed Labour Party politician, and I had gone with the intention of making him the subject of all my teenage political angst. I wasn't a Labour Party member and had no intention of ever joining, and so my plan had been to go ask him the *real* difficult questions that he couldn't *possibly* answer. In short, I had signed up to go along and be a real smart ass. As the event reached the Q&A portion of the evening, my all too excited hand was selected by the moderator to ask one question – I asked six. Told you, *smart ass.*

While I can't recall the exact questions I asked, they almost definitely ranged from covering Labour's role in creating tuition fees to the invasion of Iraq and the 'war on terror'. The one thing I do recall is my growing amazement as he began to answer my questions. Far from a 'hard man' or the combative figure he is commonly portrayed as in the British press, he calmly began to answer each of my questions. Not dodging their controversies or roots, not spinning his answers to make them palatable to mainstream positions, not denying when he believed his party had made a mistake or had got it wrong on a piece of policy, he just answered them honestly. As he moved from one answer to the next, I became simultaneously uncomfortable and optimistic. This wasn't the reaction I had expected, nor the one I had intended to get when I arrived. I had expected another template Labour politician, obfuscating and pettifogging every question; what I actually saw was someone very different. In his manner and answers, John McDonnell was fundamentally challenging a political orthodoxy I had established in my own mind: that they were all the same.

I was so profoundly struck by the 10–15 minutes of answers to my questions that I made a point to go and find our speaker at the end of the session. As the crowd began to disperse through the lecture hall and headed towards the exit, I wrestled my way through until I was stood directly beside him. We spoke for around 5 minutes, him asking about what I was studying and elaborating more on some of the questions I had asked. At the end of our conversation I remember distinctly saying to him, 'I'm not a member of the Labour Party and have never even considered joining, but I want to campaign for you in the next election.' He smiled, thanked me and passed on his contact information, urging me to stay in touch over the course of my study. It would take me two more years to join the Labour Party, following a crushing general election defeat in 2015, but no doubt it was that single experience with John that inspired me to do it.

In the years since that interaction, I stayed in touch with John, seeking his advice, attending his talks and even meeting him one-on-one on several occasions. He had built a reputation in the university and beyond for making himself available to young activists in the area, a privilege I often took advantage of. I would go on to be elected as the Students' Union President at Brunel University, a Vice-President of the NUS and then a local councillor in his constituency of Hayes and Harlington. So when I approached him with the idea of running in Uxbridge and South Ruislip, at least to him, the idea probably wasn't as far-fetched as it was to me. If I was looking for a definitive answer to the question of whether or not I should run, I didn't get it from John. Not wanting to interfere with the selection process of another CLP, he steered his advice to me to the broader question of whether or not I *could* be a Labour candidate. In that he was clear – the party desperately needed more young voices with a campaigning background, more people from within the community and those who understood what life was like for its constituents. As far as he was concerned, it wasn't a question of *if* people like me could be candidates, but one of when our party would begin embracing us as candidates.

As I broadened my consultation with other members, I found this theme to be really powerful. Members weren't just warm to the idea of me running, but openly enthusiastic. I spoke to Peter Curling, a councillor in Hillingdon and leader of the local Labour group, who told me explicitly he would support my candidacy. His view was that our local party needed a candidate with a real 'campaign energy' and someone who knew the local area and its issues well. I spoke with Jane and Andy Smith – two longstanding local party members I had hardly known prior to reaching out – and they equally spoke of the need to get a younger, local face involved in the selection process, having previously had a candidate from outside the constituency imposed on them. Norrette Moore thought there could be an incredible poetry to my candidacy, being a young Muslim immigrant standing against Boris Johnson. Suffice to say, the reaction I got from the few local members I spoke to was totally unexpected. They hadn't all said they would support me, but all seemed at least somewhat excited by the prospect of a different kind of candidate standing.

Even with the support and positive message from John McDonnell and local members, I still didn't feel ready. I had not yet climbed to the peak of my own self-constructed mountain. I could not yet see myself standing as a candidate for this far-away Houses of Parliament. I made one last decision – I would host a meeting with local young people and see what they thought. I knew that, first, to even have a chance of not being embarrassed in the primary election I would need the support of young members, and second, if they weren't won over by the idea, how could I possibly expect anyone else to be? A few weeks before the nomination process officially opened, I invited a group of seven or eight students from Brunel University Labour Club to a local pizza restaurant. In the months prior to our meeting, I had set up a small 'pizza and politics' event every month to try and encourage more young people to engage with local politics. In an attempt to drive down the average age of our CLP meetings (which must have been north of 65), we would order a load of pizzas and host political discussion groups for anyone interested in coming along and talking about politics. It had worked – the number of young people attending our CLP meetings had rapidly risen (although getting them to come back was an altogether different challenge), and engagement in our local party began to increase too. We would all meet up before party meetings, grab some pizza and walk across to the CLP event together; the group, in a very short space of time, had become a really close-knit unit that I had been proud to facilitate.

Crammed into the corner of a pizza restaurant in Uxbridge town centre, we spent a fair amount of time in our normal routine – discussing everything from contemporary political issues, to funny gaffes we had seen in politician media appearances, to moments of history that we found fascinating. The conversation went on a while before I brought up my potential candidacy — largely due to my anxiety of being ridiculed by my own peers. I finally plucked up the courage and presented the idea to the group as a whole. I explained why I was considering running, what kind of campaign I believed we could run, and that a few local people had already expressed their support. I ended my speech by explaining that we almost definitely wouldn't win, but if people around the table thought it was worth getting a young, BAME, working-class voice in the election, I would think about doing it alongside them. The response of the table made me emotional. Instantly the mood changed. A palpable sense of excitement and optimism took over the group. They weren't just open to the prospect of me standing, but exhilarated by the prospect and raring to get going. I got a simple message from the group as a whole: I had to do it. As we finished off our dessert, one particular member said something that made up my mind for me. Cayla Martin, a long-time local activist who had worked with me in getting more of us involved in the CLP, turned to me and said, 'You can't always be telling all these guys to get more involved, engage in local elections and then not stand yourself. You at least owe it to them to try.'

Cayla was right. I had put myself through a rollercoaster experience to even consider standing. I immediately became conscious of the fact that a Boris Johnson or a David Cameron or any of their peers coming from Eton and Oxbridge would have never needed this many voices to convince them to run. They wouldn't place barrier on barrier in front of themselves. They wouldn't believe themselves to be too young, too inexperienced or too unworthy. For them, these positions were made for them. And if that was the case for them, why not for us too?

As I digested Cayla's words, my mind was taken back to my own family. To my mum's sacrifice all those years ago, travelling across oceans for a new world. To the blind faith she had and the courage to step on that plane and embrace a new world and a new life for her children. If that courage existed in her, then maybe it existed in me too.

Fuck it, I thought, what's the worst that could happen?

2

'Every election has a story'

Moments of real clarity are hard to come by in politics. A moment in which something you see or hear elucidates a previously foggy and grainy perspective. I had mine at the end of November 2018.

The Labour Party's elections team organised a candidates' residential for over 100 potential future MPs on 24 November 2018, all of us tasked with winning key marginal seats throughout the UK. Following the surprise results of the 2017 General Election, which saw the Conservative Party lose their overall majority in the House of Commons, it seemed another election was likely to be triggered at any given moment. With each passing day, Prime Minister Theresa May's government lost vote after vote in the House and the growing instability of the government saw us drift, like an unmanned fishing boat sailing across choppy waters, closer to a snap election. This turbulence in our politics meant that Labour – sensing a real opportunity to topple nearly a decade of Tory rule – found itself scrambling to get candidates selected, trained and embedded within hundreds of constituencies in time to be ready to fight an election at a moment's notice.

In the early days of my candidacy, I recall feeling completely unequipped. The prospect of a general election was entirely frightening. I had neither the tools nor the confidence to fight Boris Johnson, were an election to be called. And I wasn't the only one. As we approached the end of 2018, the candidate selection process had moved rapidly and attention began to descend on us all. From the eyes of the British press to expectations of local party activists, candidates from all sections of the party were feeling the pressure of the election cloud above us. The candidates' residential organised for the winter of 2018 was designed by the Labour elections team to act as somewhat of an antidote to these concerns, and to rapidly upskill the candidates pool to be election-ready.

The first (and only) candidates' residential that I attended was organised in the Crowne Plaza hotel in the heart of Nottingham. The hotel was not unlike the countless venues I had experienced in my years travelling and hosting such events with the NUS. Suffice to say, as I arrived in the venue to check in, it was not an environment I was uncomfortable in. I had become quite adept at travelling to a new part of the country, checking into a hotel room and instantly mingling in large crowds of people I had not met before.

As I approached the check-in desk on this cold November afternoon, I noticed I was one of the last people to have arrived. Most other attendee names had been checked off, and I could already feel the hum of the crowd emanating from the plenary room next door. Completing the rituals of checking my bags in, gathering the endless reading materials and the numerous agendas, I quietly approached the main conference room, placed my hand gently on the door handle and stopped. I stood there, completely still, for what felt like five minutes. I had been here before hundreds of times. I had been the keynote speaker at national conferences, hosted panels in front of thousands of attendees and even presented company decisions to openly hostile crowds, but I had always felt confident in doing so. What I felt, as a candidate for this Labour residential, was far from confidence. It was a feeling that had largely been alien to me in these settings: anxiety.

There seems to be a general anxiety dream that is experienced by people across borders, cultures and languages all around the world. It usually goes a little like this: you wake up in school or at work with a big presentation you are expected to deliver and, much to your consternation, you have absolutely nothing prepared. You are shoved onto a stage nonetheless, with the spotlight directly pointed at you, an expectant crowd eagerly waiting to hear from you, but you have nothing to say. The dream sometimes includes nudity – for all of our sakes, I'll edit that part out of this particular picture. Stood there, in the middle of Nottingham's grand Crowne Plaza hotel, my hand frozen on the door handle, I felt as though opening that door would point that same dreamed-about spotlight directly onto me. That I would walk into this conference room and stand out. That I would be found out, that I did not belong. I thought to myself that all those reasons I had listed months ago for not standing – too young, too inexperienced, not worthy enough – were about to be exposed and would surely be foremost in the mind of my colleagues and the party's machinery.

After a few moments – the exact length of which I am not sure about (but can only imagine what a passing guest or staff member was thinking) – I turned the handle and stepped inside.

The rectangular conference room had been set up in a traditional format for an event of this kind – a stage set up in the front with a speaker's podium on one side and a long table for a panel of speakers on the other. Below them, 30 to 40 round tables with bright white linen tablecloths were spaced out, each seating at least 10 attendees focused on the speakers up front, each corner of the room bookended with Labour Party merchandise and pull-up banners. I drifted inside and into a corner of the room and began to inspect the crowd, looking for someone I might recognise so that I could sit on a table with at least one friendly face. As I desperately looked around, I began to feel even more uneasy. My shoulders felt heavier and my earlier worries became exacerbated. Scanning the faces in the room, I started to notice something. There was no one here who looked like me. I was the only person of colour in the room and (at 23) easily the youngest person by what seemed to be 20 years. Not only did this room not look like the Labour Party membership we were going to represent, but it also didn't look like the communities from which we came. I would later find out that of the 99 candidates selected early on by the Labour Party in the period leading up to November, only six of us were from a minority ethnic group, none were black, and only two were below the age of 25. All of a sudden the anxieties didn't feel irrational or ill placed – I really did stand out here.

As this realisation washed over me, I felt a firm hand on my shoulder.

'Nice to see you made it, Ali', whispered a voice from beside me.

I turned to my left to see Sotez Chowdhury, a Labour Party staff member who I had gotten to know through various events and campaign activities over the years. Looking back on it now, I believe Sotez, himself from South Asian descent, in all likelihood must have seen the look of growing unease on my face and come over to reassure me. After exchanging pleasantries, I turned to him and asked the only logical question I could think of to explain what I was seeing: 'Am I missing a caucus of some kind? Where are all the black and brown folks?'

Sotez looked at me with a combination of both laughter and exhaustion. 'Looks like you are it.'

I knew then, that not only was this going to be a long weekend, but it was also going to be a long campaign. I could see for the first time with complete clarity that this party that I had committed myself and my life to had a very serious problem. The way the Labour Party was selecting its candidates across the country was clearly not working. I knew that in just a few months I, and many others, would be going to the country to ask for their support in forming the very first Labour government for a generation. Our campaign and that future government would be relying on the votes and support of millions of BAME communities, of young voters and beyond, and this collection of candidates I had just seen before me looked nothing like them.

★ ★ ★

Even compared to other major political parties across the Western world, the Labour Party's process for selecting candidates can be described as archaic, inaccessible and too often subject to controversy. It would not be unreasonable to expect a party that aims to represent ordinary working-class voices to have a simple and open process, perhaps one where party members are invited to submit their interest, are required to gather support and nominations by local constituents (with a reasonable threshold set) and then run in a local primary to determine who becomes the eventual Labour candidate.

In the US, and particularly in the Democratic Party, the process is much more straightforward. In any given district, a representative in Congress can find themselves subject to a primary challenge. All a potential candidate must have is enough signatures from voters from within the district to challenge. This process has given opportunities to the likes of Alexandria Ocasio-Cortez to challenge and win primary races against long-established Democratic Party powerhouses.

A simple process like this would be easy to understand, accessible beyond the Westminster bubble, and would give a platform to a range of talented and enthusiastic individuals – regardless of their previous experience in internal party politics. But as I and many others have learned all too well, that is just not how our party chooses to select candidates; quite the contrary, in fact. At every stage Labour has instilled bureaucratic process after bureaucratic process and has centralised the selection mechanisms, ultimately creating a system that too often locks some out while encouraging others in.

This system has come under intense scrutiny in recent years, enough scrutiny whereby in the 2020 Labour leadership election, most leadership candidates discussed the need for greater local involvement in the selection of candidates. Keir Starmer MP, the eventual winner of that race, tweeted his clear position: 'The selections for Labour candidates needs to be more democratic and we should end NEC [National Executive Council] impositions of candidates. Local Party members should select their candidates for every election.'[1]

Yet even after Keir Starmer's victory, and with his promise locked in, the Labour selection process continued to be embroiled in scandal. Selections in Hartlepool and Liverpool were shrouded in accusations of stitch-ups and anti-democratic practices as the party's NEC imposed shortlists and eliminated candidates with local support.

Overall, and outside emergency selections and extraordinary scenarios, the journey of a potential parliamentary candidate in our current Labour Party often looks something like this:

- A selection panel is established in a local constituency Labour Party (a CLP), which is chaired by an external member of the NEC and includes representatives from the local party, trade unions and local affiliates.

- Candidates are asked to submit a 'political CV' outlining all previous campaigning, trade union and public office experiences. The CV should include why the candidate wants to stand and what makes them the best candidate for the coming election, and asks that the candidate highlights any issue that may arise that may be embarrassing and/or used against Labour in an election.
- A longlist of candidates is determined by the established selection panel using these 'political CVs'.
- The longlisted candidates are then interviewed by the selection panel.
- These candidates are consequently put to organised branches (if they exist) for supportive nominations, which are non-binding and only act as an advisory to the established selection panel.
- Following interviews and nominations, the selection panel makes a judgement and narrows down the longlist to a shortlist of approved and acceptable candidates to be placed in front of the membership for a primary election.

This entire process is then also underpinned by a number of additional caveats and rules, as highlighted in the Labour Party rulebook:

1. The NEC may [at any time] establish a national parliamentary panel of candidates in the selection procedure appended to these rules.
2. The normal procedure may be dispensed with by the NEC where no valid nominations are received, or when an emergency arises, or when the NEC are of the opinion that the interests of the Party would be best served by the suspension of the procedures issued by the NEC.
3. The selection of a parliamentary candidate shall not be regarded as completed until the name of the member selected has been placed before a meeting of the NEC and her or his selection has

been endorsed. Until such endorsement has been received the member shall not be introduced to the public as a prospective candidate.[2]

What becomes clear to anyone who has either been involved in a parliamentary selection, or has studied the processes in any great detail, is that there is a clear institutional reliance on centralised control. Despite having hundreds of local constituency Labour parties operating on a daily basis, often with deep roots in their local communities and knowing full well what would win an election, it is, rather, the centralised NEC body that maintains ultimate power over candidate selections. The practice of pre-approving the list of candidates before they are presented to local members, the dispersion of all selection procedures based on the simple and vague 'opinion' of the NEC body, the need for a final NEC endorsement before candidates can be introduced to the public – all these measures and many more show an instinctual desire by the central command of the party (under many different leaders) to maintain a tight grip at every stage of the journey. The current process of selections rewards all the wrong traits and promotes many of the wrong people. It favours factional loyalty over campaigning capabilities. It promotes political hacks over political performers. I believe it has led us to a class of politicians (with some very notable exceptions) in Parliament who must be among the least talented public performers in Western democracies. So why this obsession? To some extent, it is understandable. Party officials will often make the argument that these mechanisms are critical to the 'quality control' of candidates and are methods of protecting the 'reputation of the national Labour Party'.

This is not a wholly unreasonable position to hold. They (party HQ) claim that for a major political party it is essential to put in place processes that ensure its future public officials are of the highest moral and ethical standing, and that they can withstand the public scrutiny that would come with an election campaign. Taken at face value, this is hard to disagree with. We all know the onslaught that can come the way of candidates from the British press. However, those of us who have experience with the process know there is much more to it. We know, for example, that many of these processes already exist for every member long before they seek a nomination for public office. All Labour Party members (representatives or not) are expected at all times to be of high moral and ethical standards. Thus, if someone does not meet that expectation and threshold, it is their position in the party as a whole that is in question. There is no tiered membership system in the Labour movement – you are either good enough to be a member and a representative, or you are not. It cannot be left to the judgement of individuals at party HQ to decide the scale of an individual member's worth.

We have also seen plenty of examples in recent years of abuses of power for internal factional gains – from all sides. These have been particularly true in the complaints process, where members have seen their complaints not taken seriously or their outcomes subject to the factional whims of the given individuals in power. This was so much so the case, that, in September 2021, the Labour Party was forced to introduce a new 'independent complaints system' to curb the amount of political influence in this process.

We know that with a process so tightly controlled from party HQ there are serious consequences for both the health of local democracies and the kind of candidates that we end up with. The Institute for Government explored this issue in a paper published in September 2011 titled *What works in candidate selection?*[3] On the issue of centralisation of procedures, the paper concluded that central control of the process discourages newer members from participating, and demotivates existing party members, which 'risks undermining the health of political parties as locally-rooted membership organisations.' The paper also goes on to highlight two critically important side-effects of centralisation:

1. Without the presence of strong local parties able to build networks and connections with local communities, the public may become further disengaged from the political process. As the Speaker's Conference on Parliamentary Representation concluded; "The absence of a

visible party presence in many areas tends to reinforce perceptions that the political parties nationally are irrelevant, or not listening."[4]

2. Centralisation of candidate selection is likely to benefit candidates with strong connections and networks in Westminster, rather than a strong local presence. Aspirant candidates therefore need to develop relationships in and around party HQ and Westminster to stand the greatest chance of advancement.[5]

These conclusions are precisely the impacts Labour's centralised processes are having on candidate selections around the country, and why I encountered the kind of room I did in Nottingham in late 2018. There is a reason why the current selection procedures and rules continue to see Labour selecting proportionately fewer candidates who are women (all-women shortlists aside), who are from minority ethnic backgrounds, from working-class communities, from those outside the political machinery as well as younger members. The process is overwhelming and it is inaccessible. What if you haven't had any experience of 'political CV' writing? What if you aren't as well trained for interviews as those in private schools who have had it embedded into their curriculum? What if you don't have a friend on the NEC or selection panel to vouch for you? This all requires not only a deep understanding of existing party structures, but it also benefits those with strong existing networks in Westminster and party HQ over those who are embedded within a community. In short, it works, but only for some.

Beyond these, let's kindly call them the secondary consequences of the process, there are political assertions to be made around the selection journey. There are many across the Labour and trade union movement (myself included) who will say this is all, of course, by design, that the make-up of the candidate selection process and, as a consequence, the parliamentary Labour Party, is structured in a way to ensure a particular 'kind of candidate' is allowed through.

In 1999, the Labour Party selection procedures came under intense public scrutiny and controversy during the course of the MEP (Member of the European Parliament) selections. While members voted to determine who was on the party list of candidates, it was regional committees under the control of central headquarters that determined the order in which they would be placed (essentially deciding who would and who would not become MEPs). This resulted in many complaints from the left of the party, and members more broadly, that this 'method was used as a means of removing MEPs deemed undesirable by the party leadership',[6] words that would be familiar even in today's Labour Party. In more recent years, the 2021 selection of the Liverpool mayoral candidate was engulfed in controversy as the party suspended the selection process hours before the issuing of ballots, scrapped a previously approved all-woman shortlist of candidates, and replaced them with a centrally approved list without providing explanation or clarification.[7,8]

Later on that year the party's governing body produced a longlist of one candidate for a by-election in Hartlepool, giving local members no choice on their future representative. There are countless examples like this across the party – from both the perceived left and right of the factional spectrum – where accusations of stitch-ups and the undemocratic handling of candidate selections have come to light, and many more where the evidence is undeniable. These complaints and allegations have, in the modern context, become hard to ignore, even outside the party bubble. Each Labour leader and their administration is clearly attempting to reshape the parliamentary Labour Party to look more like them, and it is time we put an end to it. Our efforts and those of the central party leaders must go into making sure these future political leaders look more like the communities from which they come, not more like Sir Keir Starmer, Jeremy Corbyn, Ed Miliband or Tony Blair.

The Labour NEC is, and has been, for as long as I can remember, a highly politicised body whose make-up and decision-making tendencies are determined by the factional control of the day. Thus the complete central control of candidate selections by this body not only leaves the party open to criticism of political stitch-ups, but also, and most importantly, often leaves us as a party missing out on finding uniquely talented political leaders buried deep within our membership.

They are out there, the future leaders of our movement, those who can lead us to the promised land. But unless we look at the way we carry out our selections, they will remain lost, buried in the membership data of party secretaries around the UK.

When looking across our sister parties and among other major political organisations throughout the Western world, it is apparent that our selection procedures are not just incompatible with our own moral standing, but also inconsistent with those of our closest allies and neighbours. In the US Democratic Party, for example, the primary process is far simpler. To become a Democratic candidate for Congress, you simply need to be at least 25 years old, get a certain number of signatures on a nomination petition and pay a filing fee. Following that process, your name is on the ballot and you are free to campaign in an open primary to win the support of your local constituents.[9] Although it is true that Democratic primary elections are far more dependent on financial variables, this more open and simple process has naturally meant that candidates from a more diverse range of backgrounds and political experiences have participated in Democratic primaries and won.

This has seen a wave of new talent shine through and lead a new generation in the Houses of Congress – names such as Jamaal Bowman, Ayanna Pressley, Ilhan Omar, Rashida Tlaib and Cori Bush dominate news bulletins and legislative priorities. The best-known name in the new squad of representatives is most certainly Alexandria Ocasio-Cortez of New York's 14th district who, in her primary election, defeated 10-term incumbent and then chair of the House Democratic caucus Joe Crowley. From the moment Alexandria was elected in New York, we have all heard the calls from Labour members and supporters to find the UK's AOC, to uncover the young, dynamic and exciting candidates of the future. Well, the truth we are having to reconcile with is, that if AOC was to run in the Labour Party selection, she would most likely have been overwhelmed by the process, excluded, disqualified or ruled out as a candidate in the bureaucracy of our party's primary process.

It is not just in the US where we find ourselves out of step. A look at a study analysing the procedures of German political parties' selection processes also shows Labour lagging behind in progressive selection processes. This shows the German Christian Democratic Party (which can be reasonably assumed to be to the right of the UK Labour Party) has a process whereby the 'fielding of candidates is a matter of the district and their final election a matter of the *Länder* [lands] assemblies of delegates. Hence it is a very decentralised way of finding the candidates. The federal executive committee formally keeps silent during the selection process.'[10] Equally, the Socialist People's Party in Denmark also has

> a strong tradition for members' democracy and internal membership ballots when selecting candidates for elections at both the local, national and European level. Consequently, all members of the party were given the chance to vote for the four top candidates among 12 members either by letter or electronic voting. The four candidates who received a majority of votes were chosen and placed on the electoral list in accordance to number of votes.[11]

It has become undeniable – particularly in more recent years – that the Labour Party's selection process is in need of serious reform. In the 2020 Labour leadership elections, we saw both major candidates Rebecca Long-Bailey and Sir Keir Starmer commit to bringing about change to the way we choose our representatives. The growing consensus across the membership seemed to be that both morally and as a means of meeting our political objectives, we must break our reliance on centralised control and the political influence of bureaucrats, and open our selections up to local member democracy. This is, as we have learned, hard to do. Not least because there is, not surprisingly, an unwillingness from elected officials who have benefited from the system in place (by running and winning) to then go on and change that process fundamentally. It requires extraordinary courage, which, I am sad to say, I feel is missing in our parliamentary Labour Party. It is my belief that one of the simplest and most urgent changes we can make is to embrace the campaign for a US Democrat-style open primaries system to replace our current process. This would see the elimination of NEC-controlled selection panels and of 'political CVs', the eradication of job-style candidate interviews, and no pre-approved list of candidates. Rather, those who have been a member of the party for a determined period would be invited to indicate their interest, gather a threshold amount of local member nomination signatures, and then run in a local primary election. This would not only bolster the health of our local party's democracy, but also introduce vital dynamism to our candidate selection process. This should not be seen as a threat to existing MPs or a risk to the reputation of the party, but as an opportunity to diversify our candidate pool. The greatest form of quality control of candidates and the protection of our party's reputation is surely the judgement of local members. They, better than anyone else, know who is best placed to run, win and represent them.

★ ★ ★

I knew, by late into the summer of 2018, that it was those local members who would give me my best shot in a primary race. And my mind was made up. After months of mental anguish, going back and forth, and consulting with countless people on whether or not I should stand in the Uxbridge and South Ruislip selection process, I decided to go for it. But all the time I had spent *thinking* about standing meant that I found myself with very little time to *actually* get moving and organise a campaign.

The chatter among the local party was that a selection timeline would be released imminently, and that the primary process would move very quickly once that timeline was published. The belief was that a general election was more likely than ever, and we needed a candidate quickly. Nervous that we would be starting way behind other candidates, my small team and I quickly gathered together a draft 'political CV' – a requirement by all candidates on their submission of interest. Having never been on the receiving end of CV writing classes, which is something I have since learned is quite common in private and grammar schools, I put together my best guess at what I thought a selection panel would want to hear and what made me unique as a candidate – my relationship with the local community, my campaigning background, my ability to speak to a diverse range of constituents and my connection with students and young people in the area. But even in those very early days of the primary race, there was a crowded field of names that had been touted to stand.

Straight off the bat, Vincent Lo was said to be the favourite. A university lecturer from Harrow, he had been the candidate imposed on our CLP in the previous snap election. Despite the undeniable resentment that had been built up by local members as a result of having someone external parachuted into the constituency, it was hard to argue against Vincent's success in the previous election. Following the surprise Labour surge across the country, the Conservative majority in Uxbridge and South Ruislip had been halved with Vincent as the Labour candidate. The seat had gone from a majority of 10,695 to just 5,034, officially flipping us from a safe Conservative constituency to a winnable marginal for Labour. Most members of the local party, including me, believed from the beginning that the selection would be a foregone conclusion and Vincent would be reselected. In my mind, I just could not see how we, or any opposing candidate, would be able to overcome the simplicity of Vincent's potential message: 'I halved his majority last time, stick with me, and next time I will unseat him altogether.'

Another name that had been floating around for some time was that of Christian Wolmar. A journalist and an author, Christian was easily the most recognisable name among those who were thinking of standing. Christian also had the advantage of being an expert on issues surrounding transport, and with the Heathrow expansion and the building of a new high-speed railway being a prominent political issue in the area, he certainly had an advantage when talking on those subjects. Like Vincent, however, he had one difficulty to overcome – he was not himself a local.

The preference among members across the party spectrum for a local candidate was undeniable. With Boris Johnson having been parachuted in by the Conservatives and having no connection with the local area, the feeling among the Labour group was that we surely could not do the same thing with our candidate. So as the weeks passed and discussions were being had between party meetings and in the corners of local pubs, there was a quiet consensus growing in the local CLP: we needed a local candidate. Among the local names that were expected to run, there were only really two who were serious contenders. The first was Jess Beishon, chair of the CLP, a governor of a local school and an active member of the community. Jess was firmly on the left of the party and would have a strong base of support behind her candidacy. The second was Steve Garelick, a taxi driver, union rep and the secretary of our neighbouring Ruislip, Northwood and Pinner CLP. Steve was someone who was both well known and well liked among Uxbridge members, and had been closely involved in the 2018 local elections. We had personally campaigned together in multiple elections prior to this primary, so his campaigning ability and commitment was never something that was in question.

It would be no exaggeration to say that in the first few weeks of the primary campaign, most members (and even my own supporters) saw me as either fourth or fifth most likely to win. That didn't bother me much. As discussed with those closest to me, I had never really believed in those early days that I was going to win the primary; my main aim was to provide a different perspective, to bring with me my young voters, BAME voters and those who don't traditionally engage with the selection of their local candidate. If I could infuse their voice into the process, I thought, then whoever did become the eventual candidate would have to make them central to their general election campaign too.

As I began to quietly express my intention to stand, I received an interesting mix of responses from the most highly engaged members – from the laughter of those who thought it was unthinkable, to the genuine excitement of those who foresaw what it might mean for our constituents and the country as a whole. If there was one emotion my candidacy didn't evoke, it was apathy. I recall one member telling me, on a warm night following a local constituency meeting, that the only way I even stood a chance was if I brought an army of students and young people with me. Because these 'old folks', as he put it, would 'never vote for a 20-something year old' to be their local candidate. An army of students and young people? Sounds like a plan, I remember thinking to myself. There was one problem, however; the numbers just did not add up. There simply weren't enough young members and students to get us over the line. To win, I had to win the support of older, traditional local Labour supporters.

It was time to start climbing that hill.

* * *

The challenge of winning over traditional, older voters within the local party never really intimidated me much. While I knew I would have a slightly more difficult challenge compared to the other candidates, my experience over the previous four years had always been a really good one in Uxbridge. My age had never really felt a particular barrier to my broader engagement within the local party. For years we had all cared for and campaigned on the same things: poverty, public services, healthcare, housing, social justice, and so much more. We fought in campaigns alongside each other, organised community actions together and sometimes argued policy among each other. To me, they were my local Labour family. Sure, it might take a little longer to get them to see me in the role of a parliamentary candidate, but I never really bought into the fact that they would 'never vote for a 20-something-year-old' as a candidate.

The greater challenge in those weeks was not what I was going to say to convince local party members to support me, but whether I would be able to talk to them at all. Uxbridge and South Ruislip had over 600 members across the constituency at the time, and local membership data, for obvious reasons, was not something that was ever shared with anyone beyond the CLP executives. This includes potential candidates. It was only once candidates made the final shortlist and were on the ballot that the party would release the member information that would allow us as candidates to email, call and deliver campaign materials. But without that membership data, we all knew that we were going to struggle to garner enough support to get on the ballot. We found ourselves in a classic catch-22.

This, in many ways, highlights the problem with our primaries. They are riddled with layer upon layer of process and procedure. Rather than allowing candidates to have a battle of ideas and to campaign in a way that readies them for a general election, we fight over data and in interview rooms. We write CVs rather than manifestos. We play the game of political hacks rather than the art of political campaigning. The process from start to end is designed for people who understand it, who have been trained in it, and who have friends in high Labour places. It can therefore be no surprise that we struggle to recruit and successfully elect candidates from a broad range of backgrounds. They see this process and either give up on it, or are unable to get through the gatekeepers.

As we scrambled around to find a way to reach party members, I received an unexpected call from an old friend at Labour HQ. Throughout my travels within the Labour movement, I have been privileged to connect with an amazing community of activists and members, thousands of people who are joined by their insatiable appetite for a better world. In this particular case, I had become close to a Labour staff member who worked at the central London Southside office, our headquarters in the capital and the heart of the party machinery. After a brief catch-up phone call, she asked me if the rumours – that I was intending to stand for selection in Uxbridge and South Ruislip – were true. I was surprised to hear that word had reached that far. Laughing at the prospect of local Uxbridge politics travelling the length of the London Underground, I answered playfully: 'Maybe, why do you ask?' Her tone quickly shifted to one of concern. Like someone who was reluctantly delivering bad news, she told me that she had heard rumours that some people in positions of power would be working on preventing me from running.

'The word is that they are going to do all that they can to stop you getting on the ballot.'

I felt my heart sink. After all I had put myself and my team through in deciding to run, and the organising work we had already embarked on locally, it felt deeply unfair to have unelected, outside influencers deciding whether or not I could stand in this primary. I had entered this race not expecting to win, but that was okay, because the final decision would come from my local community. It would be the Labour members in Uxbridge and South Ruislip who would decide whether I was a worthy enough candidate to represent them. This, in contrast, felt like a deep injustice. Why did a bureaucrat in central London think they had the power to stop our campaign? Why did they even have the (informal) power to interfere in the selection process? Like most things in my political life, that feeling of injustice quickly turned to anger, and that anger to motivation. My team and I now knew what we had to do.

Whatever it took, I had to get my name on that primary ballot.

★ ★ ★

The beginning of our primary campaign for Uxbridge and South Ruislip nomination was the definition of a grassroots guerrilla campaign. Without any membership data or an idea of where we could find Labour members in the constituency, we reverted to a tried and tested campaigning tool from our days in the student movement. I had recruited the support of some old friends – Ibrahim, a CLP local secretary, as well as Sayed and Yusuf, who I had discussed running with months prior. Using Facebook, Twitter and Instagram, we spent hours early in the mornings or late at night after work searching word combinations and public pages on social media, looking for anyone who may have posted publicly about Labour and lived within the confines of our constituency. We would then send them a message with my campaign material, why I was standing, and offer a personal conversation via a phone call or a coffee in town.

To my surprise, this method was exceptionally effective. I found myself having conversations over the phone and coffees with members from across the constituency, many of whom had never come along to a party meeting or even engaged in any of our campaigns. Sure, along the way, I was blocked by quite a few Facebook accounts and wasted hours of my time talking to people who I would find out, always at the end of the call, were neither members of the Labour Party nor lived in the area, but we were succeeding in getting me in front of voters, talking to them about my vision for this campaign, and how we were going to transform our communities together.

As I embarked on my speaking tour with members, and with the looming threat of interference from party HQ above us, our team had ransacked the party rulebook to find some way to ensure my participation in the later part of the process, to safeguard against the potential interference we had been warned against. Then, one evening, we found a saving grace. As it turns out, it is part of party rules that if any candidate receives more than half of the ward nominations of the entire constituency, they must automatically be shortlisted and their name included on the final ballot. That meant that if we were able to get five of the eight wards in Uxbridge and South Ruislip to nominate us, we would have a real chance at fighting this campaign in the latter stages.

For over a month, I spent every moment not at work searching for and speaking to local members. Anyone we could convince to support our campaign we organised according to the wards in which they lived, and stayed in touch to point them towards the eventual ward nomination meetings. It was in these conversations and having coffee with local members that I began to sense a feeling of hope. As I told them of the once-in-a-lifetime opportunity I believed we had here, in Uxbridge, with this campaign, to bring together young and old, nurses and bus drivers, working-class communities and immigrant families, I saw their faces light up. They weren't concerned about my age or experience; they believed in the power of my story. They believed that if we could do this, we could change the nature of politics in this country. What if an Ali Milani, a normal working-class kid from a council estate, who travelled to the UK as an asylum-seeker at the age of five, could go on to unseat the most recognisable face in British politics? What if he, and his story, could topple Boris Johnson? Members began to believe that the election was not really about me, but rather what we could be as a community and as a society. It was about what my story could represent. If we could win, then all things were possible in politics. We were suddenly gaining support among all demographics and ages of the party. Left and centre, young and old, they could all see what I saw. Our story was beginning to catch fire.

On one particular evening, I had met with a young mother of three in a coffee shop by the entrance of a local shopping centre in Uxbridge. She had brought her young daughter with her, as we grabbed a coffee and discussed local politics. She told me of her struggle with three young children, one of whom had severe learning difficulties and needed constant supervision. I heard in her voice the pain of being left behind, both by her local MP and British politics altogether. It broke my heart. Rather than giving her a list of policies we needed to change and laws we needed to put in place (much of which was racing through my mind), I decided to just tell her my story, the difficulties my family had had to go through, the pain my own mum had endured and the day-to-day struggles of growing up in this community. I promised her that with my candidacy, I would understand. I wouldn't always get it right or always do the right thing, but in the end, I would be on her side. She smiled and told me that for the first time in her life, she would be voting in a local Labour primary to support me. I walked home that evening feeling a cacophony of emotions. Reinvigorated to fight for families like hers, aching with the hurt that I knew she had had to go through, and hopeful that we might be able to inject some optimism back into our local politics. I walked home to find Ibrahim Ali, one of my campaign managers, at my desk continuing to make calls on my behalf late into the evening. Sitting on the bed next to him, I allowed myself, for the first time, to think it.

'You know, I think we can actually win this', I said out loud, partly to him and partly to myself.

'It went well then?' he replied, still focused on the numbers he was seeing on the spreadsheet and looking forward to the nomination meeting.

'Yeah, brilliant, but it's not just that, I think people are beginning to connect with our story and our message.'

Ibrahim broke his stare at the laptop in front of him, turned to me and smiled. I could see in his smile that he was beginning to believe too. He grabbed a piece of paper, leaned towards me and said, 'Good, now get back to work, we have calls to make.'

★ ★ ★

In my admittedly short career, I have been a candidate in six major elections. These range from running to be president of my students' union to standing for Parliament against a sitting prime minister. Throughout all of them, I have always found myself remarkably calm and collected on election day itself. While many of my team scramble and fight for every last vote, I find peace in the final days, and have always had the best night's sleep before the big day. But there is one exception. The night before the Uxbridge and South Ruislip ward nomination caucuses is the first time in my life where I did not get a moment's sleep as a result of my anxiety. Having completed my candidate's interview with the selection panel and spent nearly a month talking to hundreds of local members across the constituency, we knew we had done all that was within our power. As we got closer to the end of the campaign, we had been boosted by a number of key endorsements. The support of Peter Curling, the local Labour leader in the council, lifted my status as a real contender in the race. We had received an endorsement from the Bakers, Food and Allied Workers' Union and the support of Momentum, the internal Labour campaigning organisation. Most critically with the latter, they provided our volunteers with a list of their members in the local area to whom we could speak. Our campaign had slowly gathered that magical and intangible element in politics: momentum.

Yet my nervousness going into the nomination caucuses stemmed from the phone call I had received at the beginning of the campaign. While we had seen no evidence as yet of any interference in the primary process from party HQ, we knew it to be a distinct possibility at any point. It was no longer just about winning. I didn't want to be taken out of the race on a technicality, to be removed based on the interference or stitch-up of factionally motivated individuals located in the NEC or the Southside office. I wanted to stand and fall on my own merits as a candidate.

The only way we could do that and secure our name on the ballot was to get five out of the eight ward nominations. Each of the eight wards was only allowed to nominate two candidates, one male and one female. In typical caucus fashion, members would arrive at Hillingdon Civic Centre, be organised into large tables with their ward colleagues, and discuss and vote on their preferred candidate. Because of the nature of such an activity, the actual raw amount of support a candidate has across the constituency is irrelevant. Candidates need broad enough support geographically to ensure active supporters in each ward making the case for their candidacy. My team and I had done some mapping the night before based on the supporters we knew we had, and felt confident that we would have at least three nominations coming out of the ward caucus. In any ordinary campaign, this would have been a good result for a candidate and enough to see them onto the final ballot. We, however, needed more. We needed that magic 50 per cent.

As the meeting commenced early in the morning, I did not want to be at home. I invited Sayed and Ibrahim to have breakfast in a little cafe buried deep within the local Uxbridge Pavilions shopping centre. A Greek-run family place, I became comfortable in a little corner in the cafe that would become my home for the next 18 months. As candidates were not allowed in the caucus itself, for the first time in the campaign the result was no longer in my hands. We sat for an hour, making small talk, occasionally checking our phones for updates, and nervously checking our watches to see when the results would come through. At midday, one of our supporters called to say the caucus was over and for us to meet them at the front of Uxbridge Civic Centre. The walk from the cafe to the Civic Centre is typically five minutes; we must have done it in one. As we approached, we could clearly see our supporters were jubilant. We knew we had done well, but how well? I approached Cayla, one of our earliest supporters and someone who, in the pizza restaurant that was just behind us at that moment, had convinced me to run.

'How'd we do?' I asked, nervously.

'Seven', she replied.

'Just seven votes?' I asked, panicking that something had gone terrible wrong.

'No, seven out of the eight ward nominations. You're on the ballot.'

* * *

Saturday 29 September 2018 was selection day.

The weeks and months preceding this, my team and I had dedicated most of our lives to phoning, visiting and leafleting hundreds of members across the constituency. Bolstered with the membership data we had received once confirmed on the ballot, we had talked to everyone, from older voters who had been Labour members for over 30 years, all the way to new, younger members who had joined following the meteoric rise of Jeremy Corbyn. With each conversation and every meeting, our confidence was building. We could feel that our message was reaching a wide range of audiences, and the support we were gathering was vast. I found the selection journey both agonisingly frustrating and quite enjoyable. At each stage, I could see the problems with the process, why so many choose not to participate or drop out – the use of job-style interviews, the power of a selection panel to just dismiss candidates, the necessity for 'political CVs' as measures to judge individuals and the requirement to have both the time and financial capability to campaign for months on end. I thought to myself so often – what if I had been the single mother I had met on the campaign trail? I would not have been able to find the time or the financial resources to participate in this campaign. In fact, the only reason I was able to afford this was my position at the NUS. I could see clearer than ever before that there were just too many barriers and too many holes through which good and talented potential public servants were falling. At the same time, I was thoroughly enjoying meeting the array of voters from across the constituency. Hearing their stories and what motivated them gave me the energy to campaign on. Seeing them accept me with open arms as their possible representative not only renewed my faith in the people of our community, but also my place in British society. I could feel in my heart that, regardless of the result, we had made the right decision to stand.

The morning of primary day was bright and beautiful. The sun was beaming across Uxbridge town centre, and a reassuring warmth had taken hold of West London. Walking towards the hustings venue, I knew that our early reservation about our prospects and the belief we would finish fourth or fifth would not come to pass. We had a chance. A small one, but a chance nonetheless. Throughout the shortlisting process, both Vincent Lo and Christian Wolmar had been eliminated as candidates, largely due to the strong desire of both our members and the selection panel to choose a local candidate. Even then, I thought this harsh on Vincent in particular, whom I thought deserved at least a chance to make his case to members. The final list of names on the ballot included Jess Beishon, Steve Garelick, Sonia Adesara (a promising young doctor) and David Williams, an active and longstanding local member who had been the parliamentary candidate for Uxbridge in 1997. With Labour's historic surge in that election, David had been just 724 votes away from winning the seat. When later that year the MP for Uxbridge, Michael Shersby, had passed away, rather than reselecting David as the local candidate to fight the by-election, the party opted to impose an external candidate – Andy Slaughter – onto the local CLP. In yet another example of a central stitch-up, Labour had gone on to lose the by-election to Conservative John Randall by 3,000 votes.

Walking to Hillingdon Civic Centre, I was somewhat comforted by the prospect that no matter who won the primary, the party would be well served with their choice. Looking through the ballot I believed all of us were capable of running a strong general election campaign and that we would all make brilliant local MPs. Jess Beishon was, in my mind, the strongest competitor. A local campaigner, involved with various community projects and well known to engaged party activists, she had run a good campaign. My gut told me she was probably going to win, although if I had one ace up my sleeve, it was my candidate speech. The plan for selection day as presented to us was: we would each be invited to give a short five-minute speech, we would then take a round of questions from attending voters, and once all candidates were through, members would be allowed to vote in order of preference. Those votes would be combined with the postal votes, and all the votes would be counted immediately following the hustings. Preparing for the hustings, I was feeling good about what we could present. Public speaking had always come somewhat naturally to me, and I was confident in our message. My time in the student movement had allowed me to refine both my speechwriting skills and ability to deliver big speeches, so all being well, I knew we could finish strong. That was, until I arrived at the venue.

As I walked towards the candidates' green room, I felt a sense of chaos. As a line began to form outside the main hall, I could see the frustration and anger on the faces of everyone involved. There seemed a particular concern among my supporters. As I approached a huddle of our volunteers I was let in on the news – the Labour Party staff members who had been tasked with overseeing our selection process were checking members' names against a pre-printed electoral roll. So this meant that if your legal name did not exactly match the name on your Labour Party membership card, you weren't allowed to access the room and did not have a right to vote. A simple example of this problem is my name. My full legal name on the electoral roll would have shown up as 'Ali Reza Milani'; however, as I have been known as Ali my whole life, my Labour Party membership card simply says 'Ali Milani'. As the two didn't match, I would have been turned away at the door. Members were rightly furious. Not only was this an outrageous method of identifying potential voters, but it was clearly disproportionately affecting BAME voters, who were more likely to have middle and shortened first names. My paranoia was beginning to set in. This is it, this is how they are going to eliminate me from the process, I thought. Over half of those who had registered to support me in the selection, most of whom were either BAME or students, were told they were ineligible to vote and were turned away. Remarkably, even a member of the selection panel (the only black member of the panel) who had helped organise the entire primary process had her vote revoked.

If this wasn't overtly racist practice, it was at least clear to me that it was one of the institutional practices that disproportionately affect voters from BAME communities. When speaking to the officer in charge, I made a point to remind him that this primary election aside, did we really expect any of those voters we had just turned away to ever engage with us again? Did we expect they would help us win come a general election? I got no reply. The rules were the rules and we just had to accept it. Gathering our team in a small huddle outside the toilets on the first floor, I tried to calm everyone down. I did not want the whole process to be undermined, and had made a decision, for the good of our local party, whose volunteers and members had no involvement in these moves, to encourage everyone to continue to participate in good faith.

'Let's give it one last go, even if it isn't completely fair, and we will know at the end, if nothing else, we have run a good, honest campaign.'

I said this to the team, but it was as much for me as for everyone else. I was about to walk into a room full of voters who were now much less likely to be supportive of me.

Whether it was the chaos of the controversy that had erupted or the fact that I knew this campaign would be over in a few hours, by the time I had made it to the candidates' green room I was calm. Speaking with the other candidates, we all built up an honest comradery and made each other a promise: no matter who won, we would all go out and get behind that candidate. One by one, we were called into the room. While we couldn't hear the others' speeches, we could hear the audience's reaction – a few claps, the occasional laugh (I think that was Steve and his famous one-liners) and applause that ended every candidate's speech. As my time approached, I walked to the stage and looked out at the audience. I could instantly tell that this audience was older and whiter, and were exactly the people I had been told I could not win over, the ones too many had assumed our campaign would never reach. But throughout this journey we knew this not to be true. We *could* reach them. Their hopes and dreams and aspirations were the same as the rest of us. They were my Labour family, and if I could sell my vision of what we could do together, we would be unstoppable. With each passing beat and crescendo of my speech, I felt the audience lift with me. They were seeing what I was seeing, the hope, the optimism, the audacity of my story. We connected.

I concluded with a promise:

> My friends, I can't promise us victory – nobody can. But I can make a different promise. I will not be just another candidate, and this campaign will be like none other the country has seen. We will bring together the passion of our youth and students with the courage of our experienced activists.
>
> We will need to knock on every door, call every number, have every conversation, in every cafe and

nursery, every school and every workplace, leave no street, no lane, no alleyway untouched.

We will fight with all the energy in our souls, with all the righteous anger, the sublime solidarity and beautified hope of our movement. The hope my mother, your grandparents and this Labour Party has promised for generations. And we won't just win Uxbridge and South Ruislip; we'll win this country and wake up to the long forgotten dream of a Labour government.

If there is any doubt in the Labour Party's capacity to offer hope, this election can be the answer. Let our campaign be that hope.

Every election has a story. That story can be us.

We won in the first round of voting with 63 per cent of the vote.

3

'The imperfect candidate'

I was determined to be a different kind of candidate. I knew I would have to be.

Knocking on more doors, campaigning differently. Inspiring a new generation of local activists, organising wide-scale community events. Speaking to those who have never voted in their lives, and going into areas in the constituency our local Labour Party had not previously ventured into. The only way we would stand a chance in this election was to throw out the 'standard practice' campaign strategy and do something different. We were, after all, taking on one of the most famous names in British politics.

Our very first campaign event came within days of me winning the primary and becoming the prospective parliamentary candidate in Uxbridge and South Ruislip. Although we still had no idea when an election might be called and formal campaigning would commence, I wanted to send a message to our CLP and to all our campaigners that this was going to be an active and vibrant journey for all of us. It was going to be the fight of our lives, and the only way to win was to be different and to outwork our Conservative opponents.

Part of being different meant breaking some traditional Labour rules. The first rule we broke was to abandon, for a short time, something political hacks call 'voter-ID' campaigning.

'Voter-ID' is used internally within mainstream British political parties to refer to the process of finding and identifying how different residents are voting. In essence, you knock on local voters' doors, or ring them up at an organised phone bank, ask how they intend to vote in an upcoming election, and record that data on a data system called a 'campaign creator'. As you make your way through the constituency, over time, it gives you a complete and accurate picture of exactly who is going to vote for you and where they live. Then, when it comes to election time, you focus your best efforts to ensure they get to a ballot station. It is a simple tactic adopted by all major parties, and perhaps the most effective method of winning local elections in a short time.

While highly effective, the downside to this being the primary form of campaigning for a local party and a candidate – as I was constantly reminded by voters early on – was that local people would only ever hear from a candidate at election time, and only be asked how they were intending on voting on polling day. 'You only ever come around here when you want my vote' is a sentence all seasoned campaigners will have heard at some point on the campaign trail.

I wanted our campaign to break that cycle. I wanted local residents to know that I, like them, had a stake in this election because I was one of them. I walked the same streets, went to the same supermarkets and had sat in the same local emergency room. I wanted them to know that I wasn't just a political candidate; I was their neighbour.

Against the insistence of Labour's regional staff, we decided that our first round of campaigning events would be listening exercises. We would go out, street by street, door by door, and listen to the concerns of residents. We wouldn't ask them how they had voted or were intending to vote, we wouldn't even attempt to persuade them to vote for us; all we would do is say we were out to introduce ourselves and connect with them and to listen to them. At the same time we would organise community roundtable events titled 'Ask me anything'. This would have me book out a local hall, pub or community venue, and invite all local residents to come along and ask me anything that might be on their mind. This town hall-style event allowed us to get fruitful conversations going across the community, and to get the news rolling throughout the community that there was a local candidate who was rooted in the local community.

All of this was designed to present us as the antithesis to Boris. Boris was never seen around town, so I would do all I could to be visible and present. Boris only showed up around election time, so I would be out and about way before we asked people for a vote. Boris did not live in or know the area, so we would make it central to our campaign to let people know that this was *my* home, this was *my* community, and what was at stake was all of our collective futures.

I thought we had cracked it.

Buoyed by this localised and quite radical strategy (for Labour Party politics, at least), I immediately organised our first campaign event within days of the primary results. We would go to Hillingdon East, a ward on the most eastern part of our constituency that had not been won by Labour in years. Mostly middle-class residential houses with many multigenerational working families, it was a ward that had been won by the local Conservatives for years, although it had also had a brief history of Liberal Democrat presence. I thought it the perfect place to start our journey and to test our strategy – outside our comfort zone and in an area where my candidacy may face the greatest challenge.

The day of this first campaign event I couldn't wait to get out. Packing my rucksack full of leaflets and newsletters, I got on the bus with all the enthusiasm and nerves of my first day at school. I had run in many elections before, both local and national, but this one felt different. There was so much more on the line and so much more that would be expected of me. More than anything, I just didn't want to let anybody down.

So, excited by this inaugural campaign session, I arrived 20 minutes early to our meeting point, the corner of Long Lane and Clifton Gardens. The meeting point we had set for our campaigners was at an intersection between a quiet residential road and the high street that connected a main train station coming from central London. I wanted people to see their local Labour team out in numbers. The intersection, which was sheltered from the main road with a small strip of greenery and two-foot-high bollards, saw a lot of foot traffic from local residents. It was the main pathway to local shops and the main town centre, so there would always be someone passing us by. As I had arrived early, I set up camp by one of the bollards. Taking out all of our bright red Labour materials, leaflets, stickers and sheets, to an untrained eye it may have appeared as though I had set up a bootleg pop-up political shop.

I sat there for a while, waiting for our local activists, campaigners and members to join me for the beginning of the session. Sitting there, my mind began to drift and simulate the conversations I would soon be having with local residents. Yet, as time ticked on, I grew worried that we had yet to see signs of any of the volunteers. I looked around desperately for any sign of a potential supporter. But no one was coming.

It was a sharply sobering experience. Sitting there, all alone, as passersby questioned what I was doing or even who I was, I felt the scale of the task that lay ahead. We were going into battle with one of the most famous names in British politics, backed by some of the deepest pockets in British politics, and with all the friends needed in the British media, and here I was, alone, sitting on a bollard in Hillingdon East, surrounded by leaflets and posters and stickers, and with no army of supporters around me. The moment was overwhelming. Like standing at the base of a mountain looking up at its peak, it seemed the journey might yet be too steep. But the only way I'd know that for sure would be to start climbing.

And that had to start with a single step.

I needed a team. My experience in previous election campaigns had taught me the most effective and efficient campaign team was one that was relatively small, had a diverse range of views and experiences, and a clear understanding of how, when and where to make decisions. Ironically, while elections themselves are the embodiment of democracy, election campaigns are often paralysed when there is no agility or clear places to make decisions. So, for all of you planning to run campaigns, always remember that the key to a successful campaign is agility and efficiency. Everyone involved should know, at all times, who makes a decision, where a decision is made, and where they should go to input their views and concerns.

I wanted to put together a team that was different in views and experience to my own, and to create structures in which every member in the area could contribute to our strategy. This way we could have both an agile and efficient campaign machine and an open space for all members to get involved.

The first decision to be made was the easiest – my election agent. Every candidate, in every parliamentary constituency in the UK, is required to have an election agent. An election agent is best described as the CEO of an election campaign. They, along with the candidate, are responsible for the legalities, finances and conduct of an election campaign. They oversee the entirety of the campaign, and must sign off all materials, strategies and activities alongside the candidate.

For obvious reasons, it is a job that often requires some convincing to do. It is not the sexiest position to hold in a campaign, and also holds all the risk and legal responsibility. In my case, there was only one person I was ever going to allow to be my agent: Norrette Moore.

Norrette was everything you could want in a local party secretary and an election agent. A small woman in stature, with short curly hair and deeply focused dark eyes, she rarely uses more words than are absolutely necessary, and is always relentlessly focused on the task at hand (never allowing us to drift in meetings). Just as importantly, Norrette was an expert with the Labour Party rulebook, a skill that is like finding kryptonite. All of these skills and trades came with an overarching kindness that makes her easy to like by all who interact with her.

In a Labour Party so often divided by factions and internal local battles, Norrette was able to hold our local party together and concentrated on the priorities of the day. During the selection process, I had tried to win her support, as had others she had been close to locally, yet, despite all our best efforts and my own sense that she was inclined to support my candidacy, she would never say so publicly or even openly admit it to me in private. As the secretary of the selection committee, Norrette knew her job was to deliver an impartial and fair process, and she was never going to allow her own personal positions to influence that. It made her perfect – not just to be an election agent, but also *my* election agent.

Norrette and I are very different, and I knew that even before asking her to come aboard my team. I am always an optimist and she, a self-described realist. My instinct is always to do things differently and to break traditional rules, and hers to ensure we stayed within our boundaries and completed our previously set objectives. I would come up with new and (what I thought were) innovative ideas every day, and she was focused on their feasibility and affordability. I thought we would be a perfect match and asked her to come on board. After some time spent convincing her, and a fair few promises from me to stay in line and not to break any election rules, Norrette agreed to come on board – and thankfully she did, as a few months later I would nearly break my half of the deal (we'll get to that later...).

After Norrette came James Clouting, our local organiser. James was a relatively new member of the Labour Party who had been inspired to join following Jeremy Corbyn's leadership. Tall and thin, James spent most of his time coaching sports to local kids, and gave the rest of his time to the Labour Party. For all of James' inexperience in the party, he had one quality aspect: he was unbounded by history and tradition. His organising wasn't restricted by how we had always done things, and that was perfect for our campaign.

When I first tried to bring him onto our team as our organiser, it was met with serious opposition from party HQ. His lack of experience and training was continuously thrown at me as to why HQ would not ratify his appointment. But I put my foot down. I knew James was worth taking a chance on. He was full of enthusiasm, of ideas, and, most importantly, he knew and cared for our local community. Knowing the alternative would be the parachuting in of an external organiser from some other part of London, I made it clear that James's knowledge of our home constituency was worth twice the general experience anyone else might bring in. I suppose my insistence on taking a chance on James was in many ways because his potential to be our organiser mirrored my own candidacy – a shot in the dark, but with so much potential.

Last to join our squad were Jane and Andy Smith, a middle-aged married couple, both longstanding members of the Labour Party. Andy had been sceptical of my candidacy, not because of my ideas and capability, but because he was unsure whether the area was ready to accept a young Muslim immigrant to replace Boris Johnson – an understandable position given our post-Brexit political climate. His honesty, candour and clear-eyed analysis would be invaluable to our team. Equally, Jane's knowledge of the area and selfless work ethic would be a huge boost to our campaign.

This team of five, supported by a plethora of other local activists, would be the basis of my campaign. For nearly a year-and-a-half, we would work together closer than most families to achieve the unthinkable. I knew with this team I had assembled the very best of ideas, experience, enthusiasm and drive. I had no excuses; it was now up to me as a candidate to deliver.

It was here where I faced my most personal challenge, my own internal crisis. In those early months of the campaign, I was forced to come to terms with a daunting reality: that it wasn't my team I needed to worry about, but my own imperfections as a candidate that first had to be addressed.

★ ★ ★

When my journey into politics began, the world was very different compared with the early days of one Boris Johnson. My first interaction with mainstream politics was standing to be Vice-President of the NUS in spring 2017. Thirty years prior, in late 1987, a certain Alexander Boris de Pfeffel Johnson began his political journey by securing a job (through family connections) at *The Times*. In these intervening 30 years, the political landscape we each walked into as young men was vastly different.

Chief among the changes these years saw was the emergence and dominance of the digital space. While in 1987 the battlefield of ideas and personalities may have been in the ink printed on the sheets of *The Times*, *The Telegraph* and *The Sun*, in 2017, a new battlefield had emerged. This one lived in all our pockets, on all our desks and within touching distance of nearly every single conscious person in the country.

The new world of social media changed everything.

The dawn of social networking and digital interactions has fundamentally changed our whole political arena. For one, the way and speed in which political news is communicated, digested and perceived has rapidly changed: 'In 2012, about two in five Americans reported using social media for political purposes, and about one in three said they had encountered messages on social media promoting [an election candidate] in the month leading up to the elections.'[1] This is as true in modern-day Britain as it is in the US. Much of the political information we digest, particularly within the working-age electorate, is borne out of the algorithms at Facebook and Twitter headquarters rather than the editorial meetings of the major news organisations.

To win the fabled 'air war' in 21st-century politics, you no longer need to just win the battle on the broadsheets and broadcast screens; in this new age of politics, you must also win the battle on Facebook, Twitter, Instagram and beyond.

The first success story in this regard was the Obama campaign in 2008. In early 2007, Barack Obama was a relatively unknown state senator who had decided to run in a presidential election that included the biggest establishment names in Washington – first, Democrat Hillary Clinton and then, Republican stalwart John McCain. By 20 January 2008, Barack Obama had made history by being sworn in as the first black president in the history of the US, having won the election by nearly 200 electoral college votes and a margin of 8.5 million popular votes. The campaign was revolutionary, not just because of the identity of the candidate, but for its 'proclivity to online advocacy'.[2]

In pure numbers, the Obama campaign blew all of his opponents out of the water in both spend and footprint on social media. The campaign reached 15 different social networks, ranging from Facebook to MySpace, garnering nearly 5 million supporters. By polling day Obama had approximately 2.5 million Facebook followers, four times that of his opponent McCain, 115,000 followers on Twitter, 23 times that of his Republican rival, and people had spent 14 million hours watching campaign-related videos on Obama's YouTube channel.[3]

As a fundraising machine, Obama raised over US$639 million, mostly through the internet.[4] 'Volunteers on MyBO itself generated $30 million on 70,000 personal fundraising pages. Obama's donors made 6.5 million donations online, totalling more than $500 million. Of those 6.5 million online donations, 6 million were in increments of $100 or less. In fact, the average online donation was $80 and the average Obama donor gave more than once.'[5,6]

In more than one way, the Obama campaign changed the game. Both due to the success of the campaign and the fanfare surrounding the historic nature of the candidates involved, political operations all across the Western world sat up and took notice. It was a sea change in the way campaigns operated in the digital space. This continued through to 2016 as Americans 'named Facebook as the site they most often used for political information in the month leading up to election day 2016 than named any other site, including those of high-profile news organizations such as Fox News, CNN, and major national newspapers'.[7]

Closer to home, here in the UK we have seen the meteoric rise in influence of social media in elections and referendums. The Cambridge Analytica scandal, the use of data and digital advertisements in the Brexit referendum of 2016, and the growing threat of Russian interference in Western elections via online disinformation shows the battle has very much reached our shores.

And it's not just news and the political election machine that has changed, but also the methods of global activism. Leocadia Díaz Romero, in a chapter in the book *Social media in politics*, notes a new form of 'virtual mobilisation' by activists all around the world. Citing examples in 'the "Arab Spring", "Indignados" in Madrid, "Occupy Wall Street" in New York and the USA, "Movement Cinque Stelle" in Italy and other revolts opposing austerity measures and cuts on social policies', he identifies a radical new use of technology and digital activism to achieve decided objectives.[8] These new digital social tools not only reduce 'organisational and coordination costs', but also often 'benefit newer, resource-poor organizations.'[9]

So, while the conversation around the influence of social media and digital activism is often dominated by its role in promoting fake news, its use for surveillance and its impact on mental health (as it should be, with all those issues being hugely pertinent), its role in equalising political space for poor and less well connected constituents should also be highlighted. If done right, there is huge potential in social media having 'the capacity to strengthen civic society and consolidate democracy around the world'.[10] We have already seen this happen in many places (see, for example, the role of Facebook and Twitter in the revolutions across the Arab Spring).

In his book *Social media and everyday politics*, Tim Highfield highlights that in this new digital space,

> social media afford the opportunity for different groups, including citizens, traditional political actors and journalists, to contribute to, discuss, challenge and participate in diverse aspects of politics in a public, shared context. In doing so, social media centralise and demonstrate the overlap between different political practices and topics. If ultimately they do not lead to increased formal participation, then they still reshape and facilitate new, informal ways of political talk and action.[11]

He goes on to identify why: 'Social media, as with other preceding online platforms, provide individuals with the opportunity to post their thoughts and media content, without requiring extensive technical literacy or qualifications.'[12] For all the potential benefits, equalisations and opportunities this presents, herein also lies a problem, not just for politics in general, but also for my own personal story.

My generation was not only the first to use social media as a significant tool for news and activism, but we were also the first to grow up in a world where it is dominant. For us, in the 'birthing bloom of the web and instant messaging, we learned that we could all be authors, all published, all with our own public'.[13] For the first time in human history, the interactions between children and teenagers didn't float away as the vibrations of our voices left our atmosphere, but rather, they were etched into stone for all to see. Our conversations locked and written down; our mistakes, missteps and personal journeys weren't afforded the privacy of being contained only in the memories of those present, but rather were documented, filed and available for view by anyone, anywhere, with a cursory understanding of the internet.

The wide-scale use of social media meant that we all grew up in public. It started with Myspace, then came the likes of Bebo and BBM, and finally the constants of Facebook, Twitter and Instagram. For most of our young lives, it was these platforms where most of our social interactions took place. From flirting with girls we liked, to joking with friends, these new digital platforms were where we developed as children to teenagers, from youths to adults. What we didn't know then, and what I wish we had known, was that these were records for life. They were our wrap sheets. All of the mistakes, the missteps and the ignorances of youth were no longer confined to the four walls of our common rooms; they were now written down on un-erasable paper, out there for anyone to see.

This was a whole new world, and, as Richard Seymour aptly put it, for the first time we had a 'generation growing up in the glare of ubiquitous publicity'.[14]

★ ★ ★

There is a term I coined many years ago: 'the panic'.

'The panic' refers to that immediate feeling you experience when you see your name and picture in a negative newspaper headline. Often it involves something you may have said, done or participated in, sometimes from years and even decades ago, that has been dredged up and resurfaced by your political opponents and/or the media for all to see.

'The panic' usually has a pretty predictable process. It starts with seeing your name in a headline or online report. Sometimes you can even just tell from the amount of notifications on your Facebook, Twitter or Instagram account; other times it comes via a text or WhatsApp message. But almost always, it follows the same trajectory and evokes that same emotion. You open your phone, swing open your laptop or even switch on the TV and see your name attached to an article and often an allegation that hits you like a bullet in the chest. And your day, week and sometimes even your life is changed.

On seeing your name, there is always an immediate and sudden sense of panic. Like an emotion being physically ripped from your body, you instantly sense whatever you were feeling – be it happiness, sadness or anger – snatched out of you and replaced with fear and anxiety. An almost physically painful process. All heat drains from your body at a moment's notice and your mind goes into instant hyperdrive. Like punching a hole into a barrel full of liquid, the blood drains from your face, and a sense of cold begins at the top of your head and moves down to the soles of your feet. 'Where did this come from?' 'How am I going to explain this?' 'They've taken this out of context.' 'I was just a kid. ...' All of this in your mind, all at once, racing back and forth.

This is one of the most sincerely unpleasant and painful experiences of life in the public space.

I first experienced this in my national election at the NUS. After weeks of what had been a pretty positive and exciting campaign, I received a phone call from a member of our team to tell me a news organisation had been in touch asking us for a quote in response to some old social media comments they had found. I felt my stomach hit the ground.

'I am going to send you the screenshots they have sent us. First, we'll have to verify them, and then think about what our comment might be.'

As soon as I saw them, I knew there was no need for verification. The social media posts ranged largely from when I was 16 and 17, in college and in conversations with old school friends. They included horribly anti-Semitic jokes, a lot of comments surrounding Israel that clearly crossed the line, and some swearing at celebrities that were just inappropriate and wrong. I was embarrassed, ashamed and thoroughly disappointed in myself.

I did not need them verified because I already knew they were real and true. I recognised them. The kind of conversations, the tone and the language being used. They were ones I remembered being used in our playgrounds at school and in our sixth form common rooms. For years, myself and old school friends had looked back and cringed at the kind of comments we once thought acceptable and the things we once allowed to go unchallenged. How many of us were now comfortable with calling things 'gay' as teenagers? How many of us did not challenge the misogyny of a young women being described as 'slutty' in our classrooms? How many of us, in those playgrounds and common rooms, actually spoke up?

This is the story of so many young people in modern-day Britain. Most of the people I have met, who went to school in similar environments as mine, in urban, underfunded comprehensives, have told me they had the same experience, the same comments heard in their playgrounds, the same unchallenged tropes in their common rooms, the same lack of intervention by their educational institutions. Ilyas Nagdee, one of the most promising anti-racist activists in the country, wrote:

> Looking back, I can laugh at how stupid and misguided many of those opinions were, whether it was thinking that secret societies ran the world, or that perhaps communities like my own were predisposed to crime or tax-dodging. It was only later in life that I would become more politically aware and be provided with the tools to understand and articulate the issues of an unjust economic system, institutional racism and so on.[15]

I wish every day that someone had intervened and caught us at a younger age. Someone there to sit us down and explain the weight and impact of the words we had used. If we, as kids, knew how wrong it was, and what kind of impact calling something 'gay' might have on a colleague and friend who identified as LGBTQ+ in our classrooms, we surely would have challenged it. If we had better understood the history and weight behind the casual racist tropes we sometimes used, we would surely never have dreamed of using them. If we just understood the kind of patriarchal society that casual sexism was underpinning, we surely would have spoken up sooner.

For some in our society, like the Boris Johnsons borne out of the hallways of Eton, none of this ever posed much of a problem. For one thing, they had grown up in an age where these sorts of comments (and probably worse) were just as prevalent in their schools and playgrounds, but without the dominance of social media platforms in their lives, these errors have since vanished to only be traced by those with the strongest memories. No reasonable person believes that these older politicians did not make the mistakes that many of the younger generation have made; the difference is who was there to see and hear it.

Second, many of them, unlike us, were chiselled for public office from infancy, their image and profile carefully constructed from the earliest of ages. But for the rest of us mere mortals, the cultures and environments of early life presented a serious challenge. Without a serious and coordinated effort to embed some form of anti-racist, diverse, decolonised education system, and to assist our youngest in navigating the online spaces, these comments, tropes and traps will continue to circulate around our schools and colleges.

I was fortunate to have been afforded a unique political journey later in my life. In my early years in the student movement, I learned the full weight, history and impacts of the casual comments a teenage Ali might have used. In these spaces and rooms, with activists and teachers, mentors and elders, I was exposed to a whole new education – political education. But intervention at this later stage is far too late for most. We need to connect with young people sooner, through our national curriculum.

I wrote about this very issue for the *HuffPost* as far back as January 2017. Long before my own past social media comments were uncovered and came to light (in fact, we always believed it was because of my admissions in this article that the digging into my social media past began), I knew of the kind of culture that existed among our youth because I had been one of them:

> Growing up in a deprived part of inner London, my colleagues and I in school and college would regularly use racist, homophobic and downright anti-Semitic tropes as part of our everyday vocabulary. Now, we are embarrassed and recoil when we reflect on how some of the terms and ideas were inbuilt in our culture and went without challenge.
>
> It was only at university that they were challenged. It was in the corners of the library and in interacting with classmates that I understood their history and consequence. Make no mistake, I am deeply sorry not just for the words I once thought acceptable, but the ideas I allowed to go unchallenged.

I do, though, sincerely believe we are all better for it. We now understand the terms and phrases that we would never dream of using today; not for fear of condemnation, but because of the privilege of education. It has since inspired me (and many like me) to work tirelessly for years on anti-racism and understand the deep importance of our liberation campaigns in both fighting and educating.[16]

None of this was to be an excuse for my own shortcomings and mistakes. The comments I had made were wrong and inexcusable. After apologising to our campaign team, I made it clear that our response would have to be honest and clear. I knew too well, having faced the sharp edge of racism in my own life and political journey, that the road to rebuilding trust must start with honesty and be more than just words. Our statement following publication of the articles was that of an acknowledgement and unreserved apology. I made it clear that these comments 'do not reflect how I see the world now', and that I was involved in the NUS precisely because I wanted to 'make sure that every student has access to an education that challenges the types of words and comments we once thought acceptable'.[17]

In the months that followed, we made sure that I enrolled and participated in anti-Semitism training. I was able to take a trip to Auschwitz and Birkenau concentration camps with the Holocaust Memorial Day Trust (a truly harrowing experience everyone involved in public life should participate in), and engage with Jewish organisations across the country. In those same months, I remember being profoundly moved by the kindness of so many young Jewish students – willing to talk with me, explain the hurt and pain these comments had resurfaced, and many, simply willing to forgive me.

★ ★ ★

I was an imperfect candidate.

I knew this to be true long before I had won the primary to become the parliamentary candidate in Uxbridge and South Ruislip. I knew it to be true the moment I won the primary.

And I knew it to be true every day of my election campaign. My life trajectory was never supposed to bring me to this moment. A moment that now saw me, someone who had stepped off a plane at Heathrow airport at the age of five, who lived in a council estate in a single-parent household, who had attended an underfunded comprehensive school, ending up toe to toe with the leader of the country in the tightest election campaign against a prime minister in 100 years.

What I did not know, and what I truly never expected, was the scale to which my candidacy would expose a clash of cultures: between an old political establishment and a new social media world.

Almost as soon as our campaign began to get moving and our team was in place, opposition activists and right-wing media organisations began to search through my digital history for signs of fallibility. The old images of investigators parked outside someone's house, trawling through bins for something to use against them, had now been replaced by an anonymous figure with a laptop and a search engine. I had thought my past comments, addressed in my student days, were fair to be held accountable for. I expected them to come up again in this race, and knew that I should answer those questions. But the trawling that took place of my entire digital past went way beyond that.

Experiencing 'the panic' had become part of my weekly existence. Every new news cycle was a new round of anxiety. What was the next headline going to be?

The things that were found ranged from mildly amusing to utterly ludicrous. One piece Photoshopped a tin-foil hat on my head because I had once 'liked' a Facebook page including 9/11 conspiracy theories (I admit to having fallen into a rabbit hole of being fascinated by online conspiracies as a 13/14-year-old, and being trapped in a playlist of ludicrous YouTube videos); another had me being accused of being related to some hate preacher somewhere in the Global South because our usernames were mildly similar and we both happened to be of Iranian descent, and there was even one published in the papers of one of Britain's largest newspapers highlighting how I used to wrestle in spandex in school. Okay this one is true. No, I am not going to tell you that story.

What my campaign was slowly having to come to terms with, and what our political world is still coming to terms with today, is that this new digital world has brought with it an obliteration of the traditional understandings of public and private. This trawling through and taking screenshots of my social media posts as a child constituted a breaching of the 'normative boundaries between public and private'.[18] Growing up in this digital world had meant that I and those of my generation were no longer entitled to the private. My entire journey, including as a child, was now public. I had lost the right to grow up with privacy, to form views and opinions, to change my mind, to learn and to grow.

And I am not the only one. You need only to look around and see this struggle between an old culture and new technology. I have seen my own colleagues faced with it – Zamzam Ibrahim, a former fellow NUS officer and friend, had an off-hand tweet posted from when she was 16 ironically claiming 'boys and girls can't be friends' framed by the national press as evidence of her 'fanatical Muslim'[19] beliefs.

I have seen it go beyond politics – England footballer Phil Neville had to answer for his past social media posts when taking on the role of the Women's national coach. Music artist Stormzy also apologised for old homophobic tweets, which he described as 'unacceptable' and 'disgusting'.[20] And I have seen numerous people outside public life lose jobs and opportunities as a result of often innocuous past social media posts. This is the new struggle in our society. Yes, not everyone wants to be a celebrity, 'but every user is involved. Just by having an account, one has a public image. Just by posting a status, or answering a comment, one has a public relations strategy.'[21]

While everyone, particularly those seeking public office, must be accountable for their past comments, I found much of it cynical. Resurfacing comments of people from the ages of 14, 15 and 16 are no form of accountability; they are a new form of partisan character assassinations. As Richard Seymour identified, these digital footprints had just become a list of exploitable traits for an old political class, one in which

> political faults, or even just differences, become
> exploitable characteristics. Since no one is pure, and

since the condition of being in the social industry is that one reveals oneself constantly, then from a certain perspective our online existence is a list of exploitable traits. And when a user's exploitative traits become the basis for a new round of collective outrage, they galvanize attention, add to the flow and volatility, and thus economic value, of the social industry platforms.[22]

This new world and its impacts on our politics has already seen a significant impact on Westminster. So many of our new, young politicians entering the Houses of Parliament have their own experiences of having to answer for past social media comments – from Labour's Zarah Sultana and Apsana Begum, to young Conservative MP Dehenna Davison having to explain photos with alleged far-right activists finding their way to social media.[23] There is an undoubted clash between a new, young generation of parliamentarians having grown up in a digital world, and an old, Westminster institution that has yet to grasp this new world.

For many, however, this has all become a sport. One 'where I paint my face red and yours blue, and we cheer on our sides, and throw mud at theirs; and if it takes a cheap shot, over simplification, or political mercenary to defeat our enemies then so be it – for winning is all that matters.'[24] Some will say that perhaps this is just the new world and we will all have to get used to it. The digitalised world is here to stay, social media platforms are unlikely to relent, and this is the new norm for politics.

But I don't think so. I think we can do better.

As Ilyas Nagdee has pointed out in his observations, much of this screenshot culture is 'fuelled by hatred rather than a sense of social justice. Instead of holding the powerful to account, it feels as if they have morphed into a cynical, cyclical exercise in bad faith, a tactic of trial by media.'[25]

If we are to give in to this culture, the message is clear: 'that politics should remain the preserve of the polished careerists of old. This means those who have been groomed and prepped for politics from youth, with the wherewithal to refine their every word; or those who have the political machinery behind them to cover their tracks if they don't.'[26] It means modern British politics is a story in which only Boris Johnsons are possible, and Ali Milanis are certainly not.

As I knocked on the doors of residents through the bitterly cold winter of 2018 and in between the publication of these articles and accusations, I found something remarkable – a public that is understanding and forgiving. I found a community who overwhelmingly understand an individual's progression. They know that ideas change, people learn, and a screenshot is but a snapshot of a child, not a measure of their worth for a lifetime. That it is precisely the point of someone's education – to develop your ideas, abandon your ignorance and your prejudice, and to establish a position. To grow up.

They and I are waiting for a politics that is mature enough to balance idealism and understanding. For a political culture to get to grips with this new social world. One that understands where accountability is important, and where understanding is important. To distinguish between what can and can't be understood. I am still optimistic. I believe that people, all people, like those I met on the doorstep, still recognise the difference between dogma and common sense.

For all the arrogance of politicians and pundits, it is here that I found the public far ahead of the rest of us. They are out there, waiting for the rest of the political class to catch up with them.

4

'I think it's safe to say, I was never supposed to be an MP'

It was a cold December night in Samarra. The northern Iraqi city, which sits just 78 miles north of Baghdad, and was the home of the former capital of the Abbasid Caliphate, holds a special place in the collective story of human history. To this day this prehistoric city remains the only Islamic capital that has retained its ancient architecture and artistic relics for over 5,000 years.[1] It is one of the great wonders of our world.

On the night of 2 December 2003, Samarra added another significant moment to its long-established history. On this night the city was the location of a deadly firefight involving US military forces and Iraqi natives. Shots were fired and lives were lost. It was one of the deadliest battles following the invasion of Iraq by US-led foreign forces.

But immediately following the conflict, a different struggle ensued. Long after the helicopters cleared the horizon and the final bullet casing hit the desert floor, there was a new battle – the battle of who got to tell the story.

Fox News began its reporting of the event with the following excerpt online:

> In one of the deadliest reported firefights in Iraq since the fall of Saddam Hussein's regime, US forces killed at least 54 Iraqis and captured eight others while fending off simultaneous convoy ambushes Sunday in the northern city of Samarra.
>
> At least five US soldiers, 18 Iraqi attackers and a civilian were injured.

Just minutes later, two South Korean contractors were killed nearby in a third ambush, part of what US officials called a new campaign aimed at undermining international support for the occupation.[2]

The *New York Times*, a more liberal outlet, reported on the same event with:

American commanders vowed Monday that the killing of as many as 54 insurgents in this central Iraqi town would serve as a lesson to those fighting the United States, but Iraqis disputed the death toll and said anger against America would only rise.[3]

Al Jazeera English, the international news organisation based out of Qatar, also reported the event:

The US military has vowed to continue aggressive tactics after saying it killed 54 Iraqis following an ambush, but commanders admitted they had no proof to back up their claims. The only corpses at Samarra's hospital were those of civilians, including two elderly Iranian visitors and a child.

A top military commander acknowledged on Monday that the toll was based entirely on estimates gleaned from troop debriefings and that US soldiers had not recovered a single body from the scene of Sunday's clashes.[4]

One event, three reports. Three reports, from some of the world's most powerful news organisations, all of which were rooted in the same basic facts, yet they somehow leave readers with different impressions of what actually took place in Samarra on that December night. They leave us feeling very different about this battle.

'By selective omission, choice of words, and varying credibility ascribed to the primary source, each [report] conveys a radically different impression of what actually happened.'[5] No facts were changed and no lies were told, but given the context in which they were placed, the order in which the information was presented and the choices of what was included and what was not, readers are subtly told how to feel about the events being described. Your hand is held and you are gently walked towards a conclusion, or a feeling, or even an instinct.

This is the art of storytelling.

The importance of storytelling in politics and in campaigns is something I have known the importance of and been fairly comfortable with for most of my career. I figured out, pretty early on, that politics is at its heart a process of competing stories, the story of where we are today and where we need to go. Those who are most successful are those who can tell their story and paint a picture of where they want to go. It is perhaps the most important lesson I learned in my training years in student politics. It's not necessarily what you say that moves people, but rather the vividness in the picture you paint. More often than not, people don't remember what you said; they remember how it made them feel. This doesn't mean you should be devoid of policy and content; quite the opposite – it's about ensuring your ideas for a better world wrap into a coherent story for the future.

Dr Martin Luther King Junior didn't have a plan; he had a dream. Candidate Barack Obama didn't say 'Here is how we can'; he proclaimed, 'Yes, we can.' The Leave campaign in the 2016 EU referendum didn't publish any particulars about how wrestling control from Europe would improve the lives of citizens; they simply claimed it was time to 'Take back control.' These examples show us just how powerful effective storytelling can be in politics, and in the latter case, gave Dominic Cummings way too much confidence, but that's a story for a different book.

In the battle to tell your story, the media is one of the main canvasses to paint on. It is the platform on which you can tell your story, but it is also an area of significant risk, as it is too often a place where a story is told about you.

In the first few months of our campaign, there was very little interest in us altogether. I had expected, in the few days immediately following our primary win, for there to be a huge wave of media requests and reports. It was, after all, such a poetic story. A local Muslim immigrant who had grown up on a council estate taking on the then foreign secretary of the country. To me, it had clicks and ratings written all over it.

But as the weeks and months flew by … nothing.

All through the winter of 2018 and the early weeks of 2019, our campaign received very little, if any, national attention. It allowed our team to focus on building a real local infrastructure. James and I put together a campaign schedule that would take us through the spring and into the summer – a plan to knock on doors, deliver leaflets and organise campaign events in every district of our constituency. Norrette and I would figure out the technical sides of our operation. When would we need to file our paperwork? Who would be our nominators to get us on the ballot? How would we finance the campaign?

Jane and Andy, along with the support of many other members in our local constituency, helped us develop our leaflets and messaging. We would hold open-invite ideas sessions in local pubs where locals were invited to come in and help us develop the ideas and issues that would go on our leaflets and communications. The big story ideas were great, but we also wanted to hear about the issues at a hyper-local level – the bins, the potholes, the day-to-day issues of people on the ground.

This early quiet period of the campaign had, in hindsight, an immeasurable impact on our ability to build a strong local infrastructure. The machine was working. Our teams were out at least once a week speaking with local residents and/or delivering leaflets, I was hosting local campaign events across the constituency and our material was connecting with locals because it was written by locals.

Then, in the spring of 2019, everything changed.

My life was a pretty predictable schedule in the early parts of 2019. Go to work, come home, change and go out for a campaign event. On the weekdays, myself and James would spend a lot of our time racking up the step-o-meter by leafleting large areas of the constituency, and weekends would see us bring volunteers together to knock on doors and talk to voters directly. Sprinkled throughout all of this was the 'ask-me-anything' events I had organised, bringing voters into small, local spaces for town hall-style events.

It wasn't sexy, and it wasn't big, but we had made serious strides in just a few months. The number of volunteers we got on a weekend campaign event wasn't big either – around four or five on average – but our data showed that some of the people behind the doors we were knocking on hadn't been spoken to by a Labour candidate in nearly 10–15 years, and so, while small, our steps were having a serious impact. One particular campaign session that let us know of this impact was in the Yiewsley district, in the most southern and most working-class part of our constituency, where a middle-aged woman ran out of her house in a bathrobe to thank us for coming round. 'No one ever bothers coming down here to talk to us, they just don't bother, I am so glad to see a Labour candidate here', she said to me, in her pink fluffy robe. She took a picture of me on the road to prove to her neighbours on Facebook that we had been there, and to try and win their vote. This is how we can win, I thought, one left-behind voter at a time.

It was around this time in February 2019 that an old school friend got in touch. Now a producer at the London-based media outlet Middle East Eye (MEE), he wanted to include my campaign in a video interview series they had been running. I arrived in the West London studios for one of my first media interviews since becoming a candidate. Sat on a short stool and against a cream background, the piece ended with me being asked about the perception that my candidacy and those like me in politics are radical. I responded:

> So some in the mainstream press have gotten used to calling us "the radicals". But there is nothing radical about saying every person in this country deserves the best education in the world. There's nothing radical about defending everyone's right to free, world-class healthcare from cradle to grave. Nothing radical about the idea that workers should share in the profits of the companies they helped build.
>
> And there is absolutely nothing radical about saying kids should never have to make the choices that I and my friends made, and that's whether we'd get the train to school, or whether we'd have lunch at school.

They say it's radical to convince us it ain't possible.
It is possible. We just have to make it possible.[6]

I thought it a pretty good answer at the time, but nothing more than that. I was sat in a coffee shop near King's Cross Station when the video was published online. My phone was blowing up with notifications, text messages, emails and every other form of communication possible on a smartphone. The combination of my final answer and the dichotomy between Boris Johnson's story and my own had resonated with people in an extremely personal way. One account replied to the video with the comment, 'Good luck, we need more young people like you who have not daddy's millions and not like Boris who has no idea about how real people cope on day to day basis.'[7]

This was it. This was the story of our campaign.

The MEE story attracted quite a bit of interest from the media, most notably from *The Guardian* that wanted to do their own video feature following me around for a few days. After meeting the journalist who would be in charge of the piece – Maeve Shearlaw – and being struck by her sincerity and honesty, I agreed to a new video piece. This video was slightly longer, at five minutes, titled 'Will this young Muslim be Boris Johnson's ultimate downfall?'

The Guardian piece was much more personal, a more emotional element to my story. As the video panned to an orange and grainy picture of a five-year-old me, sandwiched between my mum and my sister, the audio of my interview could be heard:

This is the sort of antithesis to Boris, I was never supposed to be an MP. I was never supposed to run for Parliament. For us, it was just about survival. I remember those little electricity and gas meters, for us it was about can we fill that up the following week. Whereas you look at the Johnson's family: one became university minister, one is running to be prime minister, everyone has got this sort of Eton plan of where they are going to go.

I think it's safe to say I was never supposed to be an MP.[8]

This came across as deeply personal, because it was. This was really my story; we hadn't prepared what I would say anymore than we would have on the doorstep; this was, in my heart, how I felt this race. And it connected in a way I would not have imagined in my wildest dreams.

The two videos went viral across social media and the Westminster political and media bubble. Combined, they had nearly 2 million views in a matter of weeks. My social media followers increased from a mere 2,500 to over 30,000, and my inbox was full of hundreds of press and media requests.

Commentary poured in from mainstream politicians and pundits. Labour MP David Lammy commented, 'the ultimate irony of a young Muslim man pushing leaflets through letterboxes to unseat Boris Johnson is too sweet to squander. Working-class and proud, I'd be overjoyed with the chance to work with Ali Milani MP.'[9] Writer and local constituent Musa Okwonga wrote, 'my childhood constituency has never been so interesting as now'.[10] National political commentators such as Owen Jones and Ian Dunt also shared the video with their millions of followers. Suddenly, we were the talk of the town. Overnight, our campaign had been thrust from anonymity to fame. My entire life had just changed forever.

★ ★ ★

I remember when I first saw the inside world of the mainstream press.

Travelling along the A406 motorway on the way to the Southbank studios, I was full of nerves. My mind was working at a hundred miles an hour, desperately putting together lines and messaging for the upcoming TV interview. It was my first major BBC panel discussion, and while I had plenty of experience in one-on-one interviews, I had next to no experience in a panel discussion format.

I knew this format was far more dangerous and combustible. I was not just answering questions and engaging with a presenter; I would also be up against right-wing commentators whose job it was to pick apart my views and arguments. I could just see it now – the edited clips of me on YouTube, the memes across Twitter and the avalanche of ridicule that would come my way with one stray word or an inaccurate statistic.

The irony of this particular media engagement was that it was not supposed to include me. I was still working for the NUS at the time, where a row had erupted (as it seemed to every other week) over another example of institutional racism being exposed at a major university in the country. The topic had become increasingly pertinent as admissions data became public and students had begun vocalising their own experiences on social media. My colleague, who ordinarily dealt with this area of work, was unavailable, and with me being the last non-white spokesperson left in the office, I reluctantly agreed to step in and participate with just over 30 minutes to get ready.

The time between agreeing to participate and being sat in the TV studio, lights on and cameras rolling was no more than an hour. I grabbed somebody else's blazer from the coat rack, as well as a notepad and pen, and was bundled into the BBC car that had rushed over to our King's Cross office. One hand on the phone and the other scrambling lines and statistics on my notepad, my team and I did what we could to prep as we raced up the motorway. Far too quickly, we arrived at the studio.

The BBC studio is a surprisingly unassuming building. In complete contrast to the main titan headquarters in Oxford Circus, this is a far more subtle and subdued structure. Looking more like an old office building than a major TV studio, I took a deep breath and stepped inside. We were taken inside the small hallway and told to wait outside what appeared to be a corner office on the first floor. I put on my newly borrowed blazer. It was easily two sizes too small – shit.

As the door opened and we were ushered in, this corner office magically transformed into a TV studio. It was small, but it felt overwhelming. Confined and intimidating. I recognised the set instantly and the faces of those sat in the chairs – everyone was ready but me. Once a small touch of make-up was rapidly applied to my forehead (kindly hiding the perspiration of nerves) and a lapel mic was placed on this blazer that clearly belonged on someone else, I was sat down.

The interview went remarkably well. Every line I delivered landed, and my adversaries were surprisingly off the mark. As the segment went on, I knew within myself I had done well. I had dodged the bullet of ridicule and had come off besting an experienced political commentator. As the programme came to an end, I was both enormously relieved and quite proud of our whole team. But what I saw next would change everything.

When the cameras stopped rolling and all of our shoulders dropped an inch, one exchange caught my eye. The presenter reached across, grabbed one of the right-wing contributors by the wrist and leaned in to say: 'I'm so sorry it went that way, I'll give you a call later and we can talk about it?'

I was dumbfounded. I felt like a naive child who had just been exposed to the cold hard truth of adult politics. This programme was not supposed to go the way it did. While I was still sat there, the so-called 'neutral' chair as good as admitted I was not supposed to have done well. In that one exchange, it felt as though I saw the face of the establishment. This presenter, these commentators, everyone in this building, they were all in one club that I was not a member of. It was one big network, one big WhatsApp group that I and many like me were not in.

There is an example from an episode of BBC *Question Time* that I have never forgotten. For me, the moment highlights the interwoven relationships between political and media figures in the UK. During a December 2015 episode of the programme, an exchange between the host David Dimbleby and MP Jacob Rees-Mogg drew enormous laughter and applause from the audience. As Rees-Mogg discussed the amount of aeroplane noise he had heard during his stint living in West London, David Dimbleby sarcastically asked if that was during Jacob's time in the elite private college Eton. 'That's right', Rees-Mogg replied, and as the audience's applause came to a close, he went on to add, 'I was at school with your son'.[11] The quip drew the laughter and applause of both the audience and the panelists. But for me, it represented something else, something more – it was an anecdote of the establishment's networks.

I knew all of this was not a grand conspiracy. I could see it for what it was. It wasn't a case of one big group that all agreed on political priorities or even worked closely together. But their relationships, their networks, the dinners, the drinks after work, the quiet word in one's ear and/or the text message before a certain panel discussion – all those things had influence. All those things were power. And it was power that I did not have and was unlikely to ever really have.

* * *

Journalism in the UK today is an exceptionally difficult job. Everything from the dawn of the post-truth political world to the increasing influence of social media and so-called 'citizen journalists' – among other variables – means reporting in the public interest is harder now than it has been in generations.

In fact, it is only because of the exceptional work of good, honest journalists all across Britain that so many important truths have been exposed. From the bravery of Carole Cadwalladr in reporting the Facebook–Cambridge Analytica data scandal to Amelia Gentleman's exposition of the treatment of the Windrush generation, we have extraordinary journalists all across the country lifting lies, exposing truths and holding the powerful to account. These people, all of them out there, many whose names you will never hear, should be commended for the work they do in the public interest.

I say all of this because it is critical that when we discuss 'the media', both in this chapter and in our public discourse more broadly, we differentiate between journalism and the work of hundreds of hard-working, honest journalists and 'the media' as an overarching conglomerate of institutions. One is an individual, with a pen and a view; the other is a corporate machine that often holds both financial and political objectives. To talk about the BBC, or ITV, or *The Telegraph*, or any of the major media institutions in the UK is not to talk about the work of individual journalists who may work in these outlets and produce important work. Rather, it is to talk about how these major institutions act, what narratives they set, and how they influence our political agenda.

The first, and probably most important, area to look at is the ownership models of these media institutions. Follow the money.

In Britain today, just three major companies dominate 83 per cent of our national print newspaper circulation. These three companies are News UK, DMG Media and Reach plc. When we account for online readership and presence, this number edges up to five companies – News UK, DMG Media, Reach plc, *The Guardian* and *The Telegraph* – with 80 per cent of the market share.

Local newspaper circulation is no better, with 80 per cent of local newspaper titles being owned and commanded by just five companies.[12] In broadcast media, however, there is slightly more diversity in ownership and distribution share, with the BBC dominating TV viewing shares at 31 per cent, followed by ITV at 23 per cent, Channel 4 at 10 per cent and Sky at 9 per cent.

Both the BBC and Channel 4 have thus far resisted privatisation calls and maintained their public ownership models. This means that the owners of these prestigious channels continue to be the British taxpayer – while Channel 4's funding comes through commercial deals, the BBC's is funded by an annual public licence fee. ITV and Sky, on the other hand, are both privately owned, the former by STV Group and ITV plc, and the latter by US telecommunications conglomerate Comcast. Although all these broadcast outlets continue to have a strong reach and influence, they are undeniably under increasing pressure from a new wave of on-demand platforms such as Netflix and Amazon.

These ownership monopolies across print, digital and broadcast media naturally have impacts on the type of content, narrative and political priorities set by these national outlets. Let's begin with print, and News UK.

News UK is subsidiary company that is owned in its entirety by US mass media conglomerate News Corp. Here in the UK News Corp operates some of the biggest household names in the newspaper industry, including *The Sun*, *The Times* and *The Sunday Times*. On the list of their former publications also includes *News of the World*, which was entangled and ultimately wound up due in large part to a major phone hacking scandal. Among a healthy and long list of other assets, News Corp also owns the world famous *New York Post* and the financial powerhouse Dow Jones & Company.

It is, by all accounts, a titan multinational conglomerate.

The executive chair of this conglomerate group, which happens to control over a quarter of the UK newspapers reach, is the infamous Rupert Murdoch. Murdoch is a name that is well known and often feared across the British and US political scene. On more than one occasion I have received sincere advice from seasoned and experienced political operatives 'not to piss off the Murdoch press'.

While Mr Murdoch has in the past referred to himself as a libertarian, claiming to believe in 'as much individual responsibility as possible, as little government as possible, as few rules as possible',[13] he is better known for holding a much closer relationship with those on the right and centre-right of politics, particularly in the Conservative Party.

His relationship with Conservative Prime Minister Margaret Thatcher has been of particular interest, as a 'secret meeting' between the two was uncovered prior to his purchase of *The Times*. Murdoch and Thatcher allegedly met secretly 'for lunch at Chequers, on Sunday, 4 January 1981, with the specific purpose of briefing [Thatcher] about [Murdoch's] *The Times* bids, at a time when other potential buyers were showing an interest and *Times* journalists were hoping to organise a staff buyout'.[14]

The Australian-born billionaire has also been publicly supportive of two of the biggest political upsets in modern memory – the Brexit campaign and the Donald Trump presidency. The media mogul described the vote to leave the EU as 'wonderful' and likened the move to a prison break.[15] Similarly, the Donald Trump campaign and presidency has also been close to Mr Murdoch, as then White House Press Secretary Sean Spicer told NPR, 'they have been friends for a long time. ... They speak on occasion as the president does with all his friends.'[16] NPR also reported that 'Murdoch has told close associates that the nation's 45th president calls to confer frequently – as often as multiple times a week – and that he has visited the White House to meet with Trump more than once.'[17]

Former Australian Prime Minister Tony Abbott once described Murdoch as a man who has arguably 'had more impact on the wider world than any other living Australian'.[18] This is a statement that is hard to argue against. A billionaire, a media mogul and, for many, the very definition of the establishment elite.

Next in the world of print and digital media is DMG Media. DMG Media (formerly known as Associated Newspapers Ltd) is an intermediate holding company that owns the *Daily Mail*, *Mail Online*, *Mail on Sunday*, *Metro*, the *i* newspaper and, among other assets, the *New Scientist*. Sat atop the DMG Media empire is Viscount Rothermere, Jonathan Harold Esmond Vere Harmsworth. I promise you I did not make that name up.

Much like Mr Murdoch, Viscount Rothermere has also been known to be supportive of the Conservatives. He has publicly been reported to have been a supporter of former Tory Prime Minister David Cameron, and even allegedly let it be known that the *Daily Mail* should have shifted its support behind then opposition leader David Cameron over Gordon Brown.[19] He has an estimated wealth in excess of £950 million, and once joked that if he wanted a peerage to the House of Lords, he would just 'buy one like an honest man'.[20]

In 2018, according to research conducted by the Media Reform Coalition, *The Sun* and the *Daily Mail*, which are owned and controlled by DMG Media and News Corp, reached the largest numbers of people each day, 'over seven million in the case of the Sun and almost 6.5 million for the Daily Mail (although the Sun figures cover 11 different sites, compared with the Daily Mail's one)'.[21]

Together, Viscount Rothermere and Rupert Murdoch own 38.4 per cent of the entire media reach in the UK.

Finally we have Reach plc. Reach is a longstanding British newspaper and magazine publisher, which, among other assets, owns the *Daily Mirror* and *Sunday Mirror*. In February 2018, in a move that surprised many in the political world, they also purchased the *Daily Express*, *Sunday Express*, *Daily Star* and *OK!* magazine. This move caught many off-guard due to the perceived difference in editorial lines and standards between the *Daily Express* and the *Daily Mirror*, one being often associated with being to the right and the other to the left.

As highlighted by Curtis Howard in his essay titled 'Reforming the British press', the sins of Reach are not nearly the sins of News Corp, its three tabloids all run radically different editorial lines. The Daily Express is hard right and staunchly Eurosceptic, the Daily Mirror is the only Labour supporting tabloid left, and the Daily Star ... exists. What Reach PLC provide by publishing three distinct but competing nonetheless tabloids is the illusion of choice.[22]

Within this newspaper industry it is undeniable that print paper in its old form has been under significant pressure for some time. Circulation has been in substantial decline since 2015, and most papers, with the exception of *The Times*, have seen double-digit declines in sales of physical papers. Yet, despite this imminent commercial challenge, these papers still have incredible value for their owners and investors. They are still some of the most powerful organisations in setting and shaping the political agenda and narrative.

Given that 80 per cent of the written word in the national UK newspaper industry is dictated by corporations run by Murdoch, Viscount Rothermere and Reach plc, and that these organisations have undeniable impacts on the agendas of broadcast media, the outcome in the type of political conservation and influence is rather predictable.

Brexit, Donald Trump, Boris Johnson – these are all just the symptoms. The disease, in part, at least, is the endemic levels of ownership concentration in our media markets: 'This kind of concentration creates conditions in which wealthy individuals and organisations can amass huge political and economic power and distort the media landscape to suit their interests and personal views.'[23]

In broadcast news, it's a little different. While there is slightly more diversity in the ownership models across broadcast outlets, there is a different problem that is emerging – particularly for those of us in the UK. Some have called it 'Foxification', others just the 'Americanisation' of British news, but no matter what you call it, the trend is clear to see. Over the past decade, through the growing influence of multinational corporations, owners such as Murdoch, and financial pressures to produce year-on-year profits for shareholders, much of our media institutions today have begun to more closely resemble the advocacy journalism of Fox News and MSNBC.

'Advocacy journalism' is used to describe a form of reporting where 'the reporter gives an opinion or point of view and uses stories to advance an agenda'.[24] Larry Atkins, in his book *Skewed*, succinctly summarises the principles of this form of news reporting as a way to 'promote a narrative even if the facts don't fit. The host's bias can be shown through tone, choice of stories, opinions, and the way he or she interviews guests.'[25] And while it is a new(wish) trend here in the UK, it is certainly not a new concept on the whole. In fact, the use of advocacy journalism in the press to advance political priorities or to normalise ideological beliefs is as old as the press itself.

Examples are littered across history. In 1776 Thomas Paine's 'common-sense' pamphlets challenged the authority of the royal British rule and often argued for independence from its colonial grip. Benjamin Franklin's *Pennsylvania Gazette* was another outlet that often contained articles critical of colonial British rule in the Americas. Thomas Jefferson, another founding father of the United States, went as far as founding the *National Gazette* and using it to settle personal political scores by attacking then Secretary of the Treasury Alexander Hamilton and the Federalists, who favoured strong federal control over individual state's rights. Hamilton, in turn, certainly did not throw away his shot at firing back and getting his word out by publishing a plethora of essays and pamphlets and founding *The New York Post*, which still runs to this day.

Fast-forward to 2021, and research conducted by Matthew Gentzkow and Jesse Shapiro on media bias finds that this form of advocacy journalism is not only alive and well, but also continues to be particularly concerning. Their results showed that 'firms will tend to distort information to make it conform with consumers' prior beliefs'.[26] This ultimately meant that the more likely a viewer is to favour an existing given position, 'the less likely the firm becomes to print a story contradicting that position'.[27]

This is not just a question of setting political agendas and norms, but also one of reputation. In the media environment that has been created, audiences will now question the reputability of an organisation if it does not reinforce their existing worldview.

> Suppose, for example, that a newspaper reports that scientists have successfully produced cold fusion. If a consumer believes this to be highly unlikely a priori, she will rationally infer that the paper probably has poor information or exercised poor judgment in interpreting the available evidence. A media firm concerned about its reputation for accuracy will therefore be reluctant to report evidence at odds with consumers' priors, even if they believe the evidence to be true.[28]

This form of news and media has, both in our political culture and society as a whole, naturally created silos and bubbles that audiences willingly walk into based on their prior beliefs and existing worldview. In the US, those who hold more right-wing views, often from red rural states, are most likely to consume their news and information from Fox News. Those who hold more left-wing views, and often come from liberal urban cities, are more likely to consume their news from the likes of MSNBC and CNN. This has caused serious division among the electorate, as they consistently see news that not only doesn't challenge their existing worldview, but rather, reinforces it. As a result, the US electorate is as divided today as anytime since the Civil War.

In January 2021, journalist Martin Fletcher wrote in the *New Statesman* that 'right now this deeply fractured, ill-informed country needs the gradual "Foxification" of its broadcast media (and concurrent weakening of the BBC) like a proverbial hole in the head'.[29] Although, I'm sorry to say, I suspect this 'Foxification' is not coming; it's already here.

We can see this form of reporting right across the spectrum of British media today. *The Sun*, the *Daily Mail* and the *Express*, as one group of examples, clearly write and speak to a particular audience and with a particular right-wing editorial line. Equally, *The Guardian* and Channel 4, to a much lesser extent, attempt to balance that out with centre/centre-left leaning content. But these traditional outlets are being challenged by a new wave — those who want to move further and quicker.

Among them is a name you might recognise: Dominic Cummings. In a series of posts in 2004 and 2005, Cummings wrote blog posts for his then think tank, New Frontiers Foundation (as Cummings a name as you could imagine), where he called for 'three structural things that the right needs to happen in terms of communications... 1) the undermining of the BBC's credibility; 2) the creation of a Fox News equivalent/ talk radio shows/bloggers etc to shift the centre of gravity; 3) the end of the ban on TV political advertising.'[30]

On Cummings' first point, we have seen this strategy de facto come into effect as government ministers avoid BBC platforms such as Radio 4's *Today* programme and the relentless attacks on 'what Boris Johnson likes to call the "Brexit Bashing Corporation" – labelling [the BBC] the mouthpiece of the liberal metropolitan elite' and 'threatening to decriminalise non-payment of the licence fee and calling its future funding into question'.[31]

To those who pay attention, the idea that the BBC is some liberal left-leaning organisation that needs to be undermined by the right is laughable. As the premier public broadcaster in the UK with a global reach of over 400 million people a week, the positioning and impartiality of the BBC is naturally a common topic. There are very few, including myself, who do not see the enormous value of the BBC. Who wouldn't fight to defend it? But, in recent years, the concerns around its impartiality and links to the Conservative Party have only grown.

It seems that every new senior BBC appointment comes straight out of the halls of Eton, of Oxford, of the Bullingdon Club, and of the Conservative Party. Take a closer look.

The BBC chair appointed in February 2021 has donated more than £400,000 to the Conservative Party and is a former Goldman Sachs banker and adviser to Tory Chancellor Rishi Sunak.[32] The Director-General of the BBC, Tim Davie, was not only the former deputy chair of the Conservative Party in Hammersmith and Fulham, but he actually stood as Conservative candidate in local council elections in 1993 and 1994.[33,34] Sir Robbie Gibb, a member of the BBC's governing board, is a former director of communications to former Tory

Prime Minister Theresa May, and 'was on the board of a top Conservative lobbying forum'.[35]

As Owen Jones wrote for *The Guardian*, the idea that there is some left-leaning bias in the BBC 'is a clever fairytale that allows the right to police the corporation and set the wider political agenda'.[36] He goes on to argue that the BBC is actually rather 'stacked full of rightwingers':

> The chairman of the BBC Trust is Chris Patten, a former Conservative cabinet minister. The BBC's political editor, Nick Robinson, was once chairman of the Young Conservatives. His former senior political producer, Thea Rogers, became George Osborne's special advisor in 2012. Andrew Neil, the presenter of the BBC's flagship political programmes Daily Politics and This Week, is chairman of the conservative Spectator magazine.[37]

And this has all had an impact. A study by Cardiff University academics, which has funding from the BBC Trust itself, examined BBC coverage of a variety of issues, and found that 'the Conservative Party received significantly more airtime than the Labour Party. In 2012, Conservative leader and then Prime Minister David Cameron outnumbered Labour leader Ed Miliband in appearances by a factor of nearly four to one (53 to 15), and governing Conservative cabinet members and ministers outnumbered their Labour counterparts by more than four to one.'[38]

The 2019 election was equally littered with examples of Tory bias:

- After a 'dishevelled' Boris Johnson made a complete mess of placing a remembrance wreath at the cenotaph for Remembrance Sunday, BBC Breakfast switched out the footage for a similar one dating back to 2016, when Johnson was foreign secretary, laying a green wreath. The BBC later insisted the changing of the clip was an error.[39]
- During a BBC *Question Time* live interview between Boris Johnson and a broad audience, the BBC edited a clip to cut

out the audience's audible laughter at the prime minister during his answer to the a question about whether he believed it was important to tell the truth. The clip that had been edited only showed applause for Johnson.[40]

- During one of the most notorious moments in the election campaign at Whipps Cross University Hospital, Boris Johnson responded to a father who was visibly upset at Johnson using the hospital ward as a press opportunity. Boris went on to claim 'there is no press here'. Rather than highlighting the obvious lie in that statement (I mean, how did we watch the clip on every news channel if there were no press cameras?), BBC political editor Laura Kuenssberg undermined the father by tweeting that he had a history of being 'a Labour activist'.[41]
- Research by Justin Schlosberg of Birkbeck, University of London, shows how the BBC (and other TV channels) paid huge attention when the obscure former Labour MP Ian Austin endorsed the Tories.[42] Those channels paid far less attention when Ken Clarke, a political giant, suggested he would not vote Tory.[43]

Even in our campaign in Uxbridge, we had to complain multiple times to the press watchdog about the way we were reported on by the BBC. Most notably, during a closing section of a local London report on the race between Boris Johnson and myself, the presenter closed the segment by claiming that those who wanted Johnson to lose his seat would 'almost certainly be disappointed' – a claim certain to depress our voters and hit turnout.

It is undeniable that the BBC is a jewel in the crown of British political discourse. That it is incumbent on us all to protect and preserve the impartiality and reputation of the premier public broadcaster. But attempts by Johnson, Cummings and others to brand it a left, liberal organisation is so far from reality that it merits a check in by medical professionals.

The second and more important change made by Cummings in his think tank blog post is the creation of 'Fox News equivalents' across our media landscape. The introduction of whole new outlets such as GB News, 'backed by £60m from predominantly right-wing financiers',[44] programmes such as

News TV UK, financed by Rupert Murdoch and led by former Fox News executive David Rhodes, as well as existing platforms like Guido Fawkes, should concern us all. These forms of outlets, as we can see in the US, only serve to further make our political systems more divisive, more toxic and ultimately, less safe. Their sensationalist and often partisan form of reporting make the political environment subject to the likes of Donald Trump and Boris Johnson.

There are an increasing number of so-called 'news outlets' that, today, have very little interest in unbiased, straightforward reporting of events. They do not resemble the 'inverted pyramid' formula of reporting many of us have been used to, where facts are given free from the pushing of an ideological worldview. As comedian Jon Stewart once put it when describing Fox News, and this is as applicable to many other platforms today, they are organisations that promote an 'ideological agenda under the rubric of being a news organisation'.[45] There are also those, in the political realm, who wish to use these outlets, invent outlets and distort historic ones, to push their own political priorities. To further themselves, their parties and their causes.

These challenges in the media are intrinsically linked to the challenges facing our politics today. The culture, the divisiveness, the control of big money, the monopoly in ownership – all of it distorts and divides. And just as there are some in politics trying to fight back, so there are those in the media – journalists who continue to do good work, tell important stories and hold to account the powerful under difficult circumstances. They, and we, need to shift the tide.

At a time of intensifying political instability and seemingly continuous elections and referenda, we urgently need a programme of genuinely progressive reform aimed exclusively at a more fair, free, accurate, and accountable media. And if we want to lay the foundations for a media that represents the full diversity of the UK population – in relation to its opinions, its make-up, its communities, its constituent nations and indeed its divisions – then we need to take action to curb media power.[46]

Because nothing is more important to a democracy than a well-informed electorate.

★ ★ ★

In June 2019, I received a few Facebook messages from an old NUS acquaintance.

> 16:51 [Name retracted]:
> Hey Ali
> I realise this message is out of the blue but I've caught wind of Guido sniffing around attempting to dig up dirt on you, just wanted to give you a heads up.
> [Journalist's name retracted] has been messaging people asking if they have dirt on you

> Ali Milani:
> Hey mate
> thank you for the heads up – really kind of you. Comes with the territory I guess.
> is […] looking for anything specific, or just anything […] can get […] hands on?

> [Name retracted]:
> […] wanted "any dodgyness" about you, so they don't have anything specific I'm guessing
> Probably wanting to get a hit piece in response to the Guardian stuff from today

> Ali Milani:
> yeah most likely, thanks for the heads up. Tbh
> [… will] probably end up making something up lol

The first thing you lose is your name – control over your own image, your own reality. There is a sharp invasiveness to knowing there are people digging through everyone you know and everything you have done, with the sole purpose of a character assassination. As they write your name, publish stories about your life and make judgements on your character, you are left a powerless observer – with no ability to write all the wrongs, to clarify or to put things into context. As people read these stories about you, they make judgements, they decide who you are, what your worth is, and so often it's a character and a story you yourself don't recognise. It's like an out-of-body experience. Almost as if the 'Ali Milani' they speak of is not you, but some fictional character that shares your name.

I watched on as stories were written about me, lies told and truths distorted. I watched as I was called things, accused of things that no reasonable person would quietly endure. But yet, I had to sit back and take it, as my family, friends and loved ones all read things about who I supposedly was. I remember reading the comment piece of one particular story, as a chain of readers discussed where I had grown up, where I had gone to school and how I had gotten to the moment I was in. All of it was untrue. The supposed school, the area I grew up in, all of it. But I could not correct them.

This was my new reality.

The combination of *The Guardian* and MEE videos had changed the entire dynamic of our campaign. It was no longer just the scrutiny of individual voters that we needed to be wary of, but also that of the national media. As the press requests flooded into our campaign inbox, I found myself placed under a microscope and totally overwhelmed. Yes, we had done well to build an infrastructure that ran an effective ground campaign, but we had no way of dealing with this level of national attention. No way to organise, prioritise or facilitate the swathes of interview and media requests that now came our way.

At first, we attempted to draft help from party HQ. They had advised us that all requests should be sent to party HQ, where they would be able to manage them effectively and help us fulfil them in a way that was manageable. But it didn't take long for us to realise that this was not what was happening. It became apparent, quite quickly, that rather than prioritising requests and sending them our way to do, they would squash the requests altogether, often just ignoring them. Journalists would constantly get in touch with our team to say they had reached out to Labour Party HQ to organise an interview with us, but no one ever responded, or worse, they had said an interview was not possible without consulting me or my campaign team. By this point, based on my experience throughout my primary race, during this media blitz, and what had been relayed to me by friends who worked at the Labour Southside office, I was fairly confident that help was not coming from party HQ.

I spent many nights reflecting on why our relationship was often strained with HQ, why the help was just not coming. I could reach only two reasonable conclusions. The first was that our independence in the way we made decisions was angering staff members who had become accustomed to greater control over candidates and local campaigns. I would often print leaflets, send out tweets or fulfil media requests without getting permission from Southside. The second reason was far more concerning.

There was also undoubtedly a political element to our difficult relationship with party HQ. Since the moment Jeremy Corbyn had won the leadership of the Labour Party, all elements of the party had become embroiled in a factional war, a fight between the progressive left and the traditional centre. The parliamentary Labour Party (PLP) was engaged in daily briefings against their own leader, prominent Labour MPs would end up on TV undermining our own campaign, and those with influence in the party's institutions would use this power to wrestle control back from the centre.

This war was inevitably spilling into the local campaigns of candidates around the country. My relationship with John McDonnell had meant many in party HQ had marked me as an opponent of their given faction. Many of the actors, who had been in post since the Tony Blair and Gordon Brown years, had decided that, where possible, their energies and resources would be best placed elsewhere, and sometimes even engaged in active efforts to undermine our campaign.

Yet the one place this factional war could not be seen was on the ground in our campaign. Volunteers and activists from across the Labour spectrum were fighting side by side because they, better than the hacks sat in Westminster, understood the importance of the fight. We were all fighting side by side for a better world, even while others were engaged in a desperate battle for control of the party.

I, for one, wasn't interested in the internal war that was going on. My focus was Boris Johnson, and I knew we could not spend the coming months playing internal party politics. We needed to do something ourselves, I needed people I could trust.

So I drafted in the support of some old friends and colleagues. A colleague who had worked with me for nearly five years, both at the NUS and in the local council elections, agreed to come on board for free and help manage the press and media requests. In moments of peak interest, he would sift through and prioritise the incoming calls for interviews and quotes, and based on the likelihood of the message reaching our constituents, we would prioritise the fulfilment of the requests.

At the same time, I called an old colleague, James Robertson. James and I had worked together briefly through 2017 delivering training to young activists throughout the UK. We had connected instantly based on our similar beliefs in storytelling as mechanisms of political communication and movement building as the best form of campaigning. I have encountered many political communications experts in my time, both as a mainstream candidate and an activist, but James is easily the best I have ever seen. James's strength is in his ability to take ideas and policies and to bind them together in a story that connects with the intrinsic values of most people. It's like a superpower, and with the amount of attention we were now getting, we needed it.

James and I met in a cafe by Dalton Junction Station in North London one afternoon. Our plan had been to spend the whole day together and to come up with a story that would define the message of our campaign, a message that would underpin every interview, every quote, every leaflet.

As the sun began to cross the horizon, the corner of the cafe we had colonised was overflowing with post-it notes, pages of half-finished sentences and empty coffee cups. Just as frustration was beginning to set in, as we couldn't quite find the message that worked, James said it. 'You want a message that clearly defines the difference between you and Boris. And that's in your story. Where you live, went to school, where you sleep every night. You are standing because people want an MP that is one of them. People deserve leaders who understand what life is like for them.'

And there it was, what I always referred to as 'the why' of a campaign. For a message to be effective and easy to communicate, it needs to be a single sentence that connects with the intrinsic values of those you are looking to speak to. This was ours. It defined who I was as a candidate, but also who our campaign team was. It was why James (our campaign organiser) was working so hard every day. Why Norrette had sacrificed her retirement years to be my agent. Why Jane and Andy were busy inputting voter-ID data rather than sat on the beach. It was why every volunteer gave up their weekends, evenings and few hours they had free to come and campaign with us. Because they all believed that the people of Uxbridge and the UK 'deserve leaders who understand what life is like for them'.

As we refined our messaging and established a makeshift press office, the media coverage began to look good. We had interest from every major media outlet in the UK and, incredibly, many from across the world. The level of interest in a single parliamentary constituency election was completely unprecedented.

Sky News' leading political journalist, Sophy Ridge, reported on whether 'a "local working-class kid" [could] unseat Boris Johnson at the next election'.[47] US-based global news network CNN sent a camera crew and political correspondent to Uxbridge to spend the day with our campaign team and record a sit-down interview with me.[48] We then held another one-on-one interview, this time with Al Jazeera English, at Euston Station, discussing everything from Boris' past racism to Brexit. The *Mirror* ran a terrific profile piece titled 'Meet the working-class Muslim Labour candidate trying to unseat Boris Johnson.'[49] The London-based *Metro* followed with less exciting but still positive 'The Muslim immigrant "ready to beat" Boris Johnson at the polls.'[50] Anoosh Chakelian of the *New Statesman*, who I always found to be one of the brightest journalists I had interacted with, highlighted the claim that 'this seat is a battleground for the future of British politics'.[51] Even outlets such as the *Financial Times* and *Business Insider* covered our story and the possibility of Johnson losing his seat to a 24-year-old.[52,53]

But none of these stories and reports hit me in quite the same way as when I got the call from the *Washington Post*.

Founded 143 years ago, the *Washington Post* is one of the most respected newspapers on the planet and is based in the US capital, Washington DC. It is hard to breathe in the rough and tumble of an election campaign. The speed and urgency of it all means there is next to no time to stop and look around you. But I remember this moment: putting down the phone after a brief interview with *Washington Post* journalist James McAuley, and thinking of how far we had come, taking a deep breath and looking around me at what we had built. How truly unlikely this story was. I thought back to my days playing football on the green scrubland of the council estate, translating at the doctor's office for my mum who could not speak English, and saving pennies throughout the week so we could buy a sugar rush on a Sunday. The very notion that that same boy could go on to unseat a figure like Boris Johnson – just imagine the impact that would have on our politics.

★ ★ ★

Uxbridge and South Ruislip, as a constituency parliamentary election, garnered more news in the run-up to the 2019 General Election than any other seat in the country. There were headlines and special reports across the UK, the US, Germany and Denmark; I even had Japanese journalists once chase me down the road in Hillingdon East for an interview.

And yet, despite all of this coverage, much of it positive, I was always fearful of any media request.

My anxiety in dealing with the media ran deeper than that of a traditional political candidate. It was more than a campaign being thrust into mainstream discourse grappling with its newfound notoriety. There was a different element I had to contend with: I was a Muslim immigrant challenging one of British politics' main establishment figures. While that story was a poetic and enticing one for many, it was also what would undeniably make me a target.

Even in the summer of 2019, as a 24-year-old upstart candidate, I was well aware of institutional Islamophobia in the British press. It terrified me. I did not need to have the experience of fame or notability to know what was coming; I had seen it my whole life – the headlines, the commentary, the constant ticker tape of sensationalist stories and ignorance in coverage. I was a child of the post-'war on terror' world, and in this world, Muslims were fair game.

The Islamophobia that is deeply rooted in the way Muslims are reported on in modern Britain is, by now, well established. The Centre for Media Monitoring's (CfMM) research has shown that over one-third of all articles on Islam or Muslims contained misrepresentation and/or generalisations; 59 per cent of all articles associated Muslims or Islam with negative behaviours – the *Mail on Sunday* is the worst offender, with an astonishing 78 per cent of articles on Muslims associated with negative behaviours.[54]

On broadcast media, 43 per cent of reports associated Muslims or Islam with negative behaviours or aspects, 22 per cent misrepresented any aspect of Muslim behaviour, belief or identity, and 10 per cent of images and headlines depict Muslims/Islam in an unfair and/or incorrect manner, as it pertains to the story.

Fifty-three per cent of Sky News broadcasts have been found to associate Muslims or Islam with negative aspects or behaviours. A primary example of this, as highlighted in the CfMM 2018 quarterly report, is the Sky News coverage of the Huddersfield grooming case. Sky News' North of England correspondent Gerard Tubb reported on the case where 20 men had been found guilty of the rape and abuse of 15 girls between 2004 and 2011.[55] As CfMM points out, 'the faith of these men became wrongly associated with the crime'.[56]

> This is predominantly a problem from the Muslim community. These were not people who worshipped at mosques, most of them had extensive histories of crimes, violence, drugs, et cetera. They were not all Muslim but they were from a Muslim community and almost all of the victims were young, vulnerable white girls.[57]

While the reporter detailed the perpetrators' 'histories of crimes, violence, and drugs', an emphasis was nonetheless placed on their Muslim faith and the 'Muslim community' they came from in tandem with the white heritage of the abused girls. This is a clear example of what Shamim Miah has described as the 'dominance of cultural repertoire' when discussing crimes committed by those of non-white heritage.[58,59]

But the truth is that most of us in the Muslim community have never needed these statistics to tell us something is wrong; we have felt the Islamophobia in the media all our lives. We have seen the headlines:

'British Muslims are killing our troops' – *Express*, 26 February 2009.[60]

'Brit kids forced to eat halal school dinners' – *Daily Star*, 6 August 2010.[61]

'Muslim plot to kill Pope' – *Express*, 18 September 2010.[62]

'Muslims tell British: Go to hell' – *Express*, 4 November 2010.[63]

'PM: UK Muslims helping Jihadis' – *Daily Mail*, June 2015.[64]

'1 in 5 Brit Muslims' sympathy for Jihadis' – *The Sun*, November 2015.[65]

'MPs' anger as Christian girl forced into Muslim foster care' – *Daily Mail*, August 2017.[66]

Take, as another example, former BBC *Today* programme editor Rod Liddle's reply to the question posed by the *Evening Standard*, of 'whether or not Islam is good for London', just one of the many articles in the British press that align Islam with barbarism:

Islam is masochistic, homophobic and a totalitarian regime. It is a fascistic, bigoted and medieval religion. I have plenty of friends who are Muslims and I

know other Muslims I don't get along with. I may
be Islamophobic but I am not against the religion.
As long as we're able to say what we think about
Islam and Muslims without fear of censorship, being
accused of racism or having our heads cut off then
we're heading in the right direction.[67]

There are so many more examples. So many headlines, articles,
broadcast reports, radio presentations – all of which together
show us that the problem is not a small one. It is not a question
of a few bad cases, or even a few bad publications, but the
level of Islamophobia in the British press is endemic and it
is institutional. Professor Justin Lewis from the School of
Journalism at Cardiff University found that 'the five adjectives
that we found most commonly used in relation to Muslims
were in order: radical, fanatical, fundamentalist, extremist and
militant.'[68] Additionally, Professor Lewis's research found that:

[In] 34% of stories we have found Muslims were
specifically linked to the threat of terrorism, 26%
of stories suggested that Islam was either dangerous,
backwards or irrational. Now there were stories,
I mean 17% of stories, talked about Islam as part
of a multicultural society, but it is clearly a much
smaller number. And you know the next biggest
idea that we found in stories was the idea of the
clash of civilization, between Islam and the west;
14% of stories. 9% talked about Islam as a threat to
the British way of life. So the negative stories very
clearly outweigh the positive stories by some degree.[69]

This view was shared by Elizabeth Poole, whose 'extensive
research in the field identifies the links between the construction
of Muslims with the general construction of minority ethnic
groups in the media that are largely represented within a negative
conflictual framework overshadowed by racialised tropes relating
to crime, violence and immigration.'[70]

My anxieties on how Islamophobia would underpin some of
my treatment by the press was not misplaced. Over the course

of the campaign, and as our prominence grew, headlines began to appear that were either completely untrue, totally out of context or just clear partisan attempts at character assassination. And many of them had familiar narratives. Here are just some of my own favourites.

The Sun wrote an article in 2019 claiming that in an interview for Press TV, I had repeated claims that 'Al Qaeda were not responsible for the devastation'[71] of the 9/11 attacks. They never sourced a video or transcript of this so-called Press TV interview, because it was categorically not true.

They also published a double hit piece on Zarah Sultana (future Coventry Labour MP) and myself, with the headline: 'Dirty secret: Two wannabe Labour MPs exposed as "supporters of campaign group that praised Jihadi John".'[72] The article was in reference to an open letter Zarah and I had signed as student activists, resisting the NUS leadership decision to cancel a speaker's tour because of the involvement of the Muslim organisation CAGE. Anyone who had bothered to read the letter would have seen that the condemnation was of the manner in which the NUS handled the situation and the underlying Islamophobia. There is nothing in the letter that lends support or praise to 'Jihadi John', or even explicit organisational support for CAGE.

Guido Fawkes, which had become strangely obsessed with me, had written that the largest single donor of my campaign was someone they alleged 'ranted on stage at Labour conference about anti-Semitism claims being smears orchestrated by the Israeli embassy.'[73] The only problem was the person they had alleged had not only been someone I had never heard of, but also someone our campaign had never accepted a donation from – something they might have known if they had been in touch to corroborate their 'story'.

In a comment article in the *Metro* (published in 2018), Miranda Larbi used examples of my past and well-documented social media comments as a teenager as an example of how 'we're willing to hold people of colour up as heroes without much scrutiny'.[74] She goes on to assert that there is 'undoubtedly a problem with anti-Semitism among Muslim communities in this country'.[75] This one is less a question of fact-checking and more of irreconcilable stupidity. To claim that minority ethnic groups in the public eye are held up as heroes without much scrutiny, or to imply that anti-Semitism was somehow a particular problem among Muslims, was offensive. When I reached out to the *Metro* to write a response, they refused to publish. 'Good luck with it in another publication' was what I was told.

It was always the same. The narratives and threads that ran through so many of the articles and so many of the comments were always quite consistent. Questions about my loyalty to Britain. Stirring up anxieties around my commitment to security. Attempts to make me look sympathetic to terrorism or to place me in close proximity with those who were. It was, at times, exhausting. We had opportunities throughout the campaign to begin legal action on a number of stories published, but I always landed on the same conclusion: it would all be a distraction. This was the culture that had become normal in British politics, and if we were to fight against it, it wouldn't be in a court room.

These experiences, as well as their general narrative and the manner in which they reported on the most vulnerable in our society, were why we developed a rule in the campaign not to work with *The Sun*, the *Daily Mail* or the *Express*. It is a position that I believe reasonable and moral for any progressive politician in the country. The kind of narratives these outlets distribute, the way they talk about the most vulnerable in our society – migrants, refugees, people of colour – and often their relentless partisanship makes participation with them a fool's errand. The truth is these platforms are often less news, more relentless partisan propaganda delivery systems. They will write about you – of that you have no control – but to engage with them in good faith would be to voluntarily put on a blindfold and walk into a lion's den.

I felt this fear every day of the campaign. For over a year, I woke up every morning in a sweat, turning over and looking at my phone with complete dread, the anxiety of what might be printed next, knowing that I was stood on a glass floor that may shatter at any point.

This presented a challenge later on when we were approached by Ian Birrell about a possible profile piece for the *Mail on*

Sunday. Ian is one of the most notable and well-respected journalists on the UK political scene. He has reported as a foreign correspondent all across the world, including in North Korea, Russia, Haiti and Syria. He has also won numerous awards, including the Orwell Prize, for his freelance exposé on the treatment of autistic children in the care of the NHS.[76] His credentials could not be questioned.

But Ian is also a former speechwriter for Conservative Prime Minister David Cameron, and so, when he approached me with the idea of doing a profile piece for the *Mail on Sunday*, I was sceptical. We discussed the idea at great length. I asked if he would consider doing the piece for another publication, to which he explained doing it for the *Mail* was the very point of the piece. He wanted their readers to get my perspective in a way they would not normally. He explained that his relationship with the editors meant they would not interfere with what he wrote, and the piece would be his.

He was right. I could see how this piece would reach people in Uxbridge and South Ruislip I may have struggled to break through to – those traditional Conservative voters who were unsure about Boris Johnson. Those who, despite historical political allegiances, may want a local MP above all else.

Throughout the course of my conversations with Ian, I never doubted his sincerity in wanting to do a straight and honest profile interview with me. That wasn't in question. It was whether I could bring myself to work with a *Daily Mail* and *Mail on Sunday* newspaper that had had so many accusations of racism, homophobia and sexism, a paper that would publish headlines such as 'One out of every five killers is an immigrant'.[77] An outlet that had published a front-page headline of two women leading the country discussing the most pressing political issue as 'Never mind Brexit, who won legs-it', referring to their appearance and their legs in particular.[78]

And it is not just my personal discomfort with their reporting. The *Daily Mail*, along with *The Sun*, has been singled out by the European Commission against Racism and Intolerance for 'offensive, discriminatory and provocative terminology'.[79] They noted in particular that 'fuelling prejudice against Muslims shows a reckless disregard, not only for the dignity of the great majority of Muslims in the United Kingdom, but also for their safety'.[80]

I could not do it. For all the political benefits it might have brought our campaign, I simply could not look these communities in the eye and say it was worth engaging with an organisation that has treated them the way it has for a few more votes. Our campaign was the antithesis of all of this. Our job was to send a message to Westminster and to the country that we could do it differently, that a story like ours was possible.

And that story was not going to be told on the pages of the *Mail on Sunday*. It would be told by us, on the ground, speaking to real people.

5

'Where are you *really* from?'

Keep this up. You might get hurt. We know where you are.

This note came through my door the day before Sunday 21 July 2019. By the time I received it, I had become used to these sorts of death threats. Our campaign had exploded into the spotlight, and it had brought with it a slew of hate and threats. Mostly on social media, occasionally by mail to the local Labour office, they always centred round the same thing:

> Ali Milani of the Labour grooming gang alliance and terrorist lovin' nonce party.
> How the hell can an immigrant have any say in our politics and our country
> I hope your family are well protected if you do this [campaign against Boris]

But there was one that caused more alarm than the rest. Our team had organised a big campaign launch for 21 July to capitalise on the momentum behind our race. The recent publicity had seen our supporter base grow exponentially and our door-knocking sessions had gone from having three to four campaigners to nearly ten times that per session. The idea was that a major campaign rally, followed by a mass campaigning session, would lift our local volunteers and allow us to cover major ground in a single day.

There was also the factor of our opponent's impending premiership.

As Brexit had sunk its talons into all aspects of British politics, Westminster was paralysed. Parliament and the government struggled to define what an exit from the EU would actually look like, and Theresa May's tenure as prime minister was on a rapid descent. Beyond the slogans on the sides of buses, the job now was to actualise what an exit would look like, and as Prime Minister May would find out, that was an area no one could agree on.

After losing vote after vote in the Commons, and unable to resolve the Brexit deadlock, May resigned and a new leadership race was called in the Conservative Party. For the second time in as many years, Conservative MPs and party members would choose who the prime minister of the country would be.

The race itself was a foregone conclusion – as most Conservative leadership races are. It was apparent from the outset that Boris Johnson, chief campaigner for the Leave campaign in the EU referendum, would be handed the reins to attempt to unblock Brexit in the Commons.

By the weekend of 20 July it had become clear – Boris Johnson was going to be the next prime minister of the UK. The game had just changed. This was no longer just a race against a celebrity politician, it was no longer just a campaign to win for local residents and send a message to Westminster; this was now history in the making. The job was now to become the first political challenger to unseat a sitting prime minister in the history of British politics.

It was now: local, Muslim, working-class immigrant Ali Milani vs Prime Minister Boris Johnson.

The campaign launch, titled 'Unseat Boris Johnson', would be organised with the support of Momentum (the successor group to the Corbyn leadership campaign) and attended by national names such as prominent journalist Owen Jones, Shadow Home Secretary Diane Abbott and Shadow Justice Secretary Richard Burgon. We hosted the event two days before Boris's coronation, on the steps of the Hillingdon Civic Centre, the building where Boris held his constituency surgeries.

This was our show of strength – we were parking our tanks on his front lawn.

As adverts for the event went out and media coverage rained down, a sudden burst of hate mail and threats flew our way.

The same sort of messages, but with a renewed vigour. The messages and comments had a venom to them we hadn't seen before. It naturally alarmed our team, particularly my agent Norrette, who had a sense for these things. She believed this went beyond our normal social media replies; for her, this felt like more.

The morning of Saturday 20 July (the day before our launch event) I woke up to a letter at my front door. The white envelope was the size of a small A5 leaflet and was largely blank, with just my name, 'Ali Milani', handwritten across the front. No address, no stamp, nothing else. As I opened it and took out the note, I realised it was yet another death threat.

My instinct was to react the same way I always did to seeing these comments on social media – pay no attention to them and don't let them get to me. But as I placed the note on my desk and walked back towards the kitchen, it suddenly struck me. I walked back the three paces to my desk and glanced again at the front of the envelope. This letter had no address and no stamp. It could not have been mailed out to me. This person had walked up to my door in the morning, and personally delivered this threat through my letterbox. Okay, I thought, maybe this one was serious.

My mind was immediately drawn to Jo Cox. Jo was the brilliant Labour MP for Batley and Spen, who I had known for her amazing work with Syrian refugees. Her story had a tragic ending, as she had been murdered a few years earlier by a far-right, neo-Nazi constituent in West Yorkshire. Jo's murder was devastating and had shaken us all to the core.

With a huge campaign event coming up in 24 hours, and with months to come of running against the likes of Boris Johnson, I feared something similar happening to me.

That morning I called Labour Party HQ to report what had happened and to ask what I should do next. For the first time, I was fearing for my safety as a candidate and I had expected the party to step in and provide support. I was to be disappointed. My conversation with my dedicated regional representative as a candidate lasted less than five minutes. I was told quite simply that they were not able to deal with this sort of thing and that I'd be best calling the police directly.

I could not believe it. This was the party I had been fighting for with all my life and energy, essentially telling me I was on my own. Even if they had been right, that only the police could deal with a situation like this, the fact that Party HQ had no way of better supporting candidates through processes like this – just a few years after losing Jo – astounded me. Speaking to the police later that day was not much more reassuring. They let us know that officers would investigate and that there would be a patrol car nearby for tomorrow's rally, but it was nothing to reassure us against the threat.

My last phone call that day would be to an old friend who had supported me throughout the primary and the campaign. Yusuf Hassan had agreed to come and help us set up the rally, and I talked through the threat with him. 'If someone was to walk up to me during my speech tomorrow, through the crowd and to the front, and that person was to pull out a knife and stab me, how on earth would we be able to stop it?' I asked. 'You wouldn't', he replied, in his usual blunt and honest way. A short silence ensued. 'So if the person who dropped this note today was to show up tomorrow morning, walk through the crowd and up to me, just to stab me, for example, what would we do?'

'Well, most likely, you'd get stabbed.'

Well that's reassuring, I thought.

★ ★ ★

I guess I was pretty naive.

Race was always going to play a significant role in this. The mere identity, history and existence of the two main candidates made it impossible for it not to be. As I understand it to this day, I was the only candidate not from the Shadow Cabinet to have police at my rallies and plain-clothed officers at my campaign events as a result of the racist threats we had received.

Even so, during the primary, and as the election began to reach new heights, I believed that our story would eventually become more than just 'a Muslim, immigrant takes on Prime Minister Boris Johnson'. It was part of my journey, an important part, and we never ran away from it, but it was not the only dimension to our story. I wanted this to also be about a local candidate against someone I believed to be a national charlatan. I wanted it to be about the state of our healthcare system and our local hospital, about our local schools and colleges in Uxbridge and South Ruislip, about the scandal of our housing crisis and the rise in homelessness, visible with even a short stroll through our town centre.

These things were as big a part of my story as my racial identity and migration to the UK. My mum had been made homeless as the cruel arm of austerity gripped the UK under the coalition government. I had known the struggles of our local Hillingdon Hospital as I had had to be admitted there on and off for five months in 2017. My years as a student representative at Brunel University had shown me first-hand the impact that cuts and marketisation were having on the quality and accessibility of education for the working class. All of this was also my story.

And it was the story of the faces behind the doors we knocked on. We had seen just how effective connecting with local voters on local issues had been. In the months since my selection, by far the most effective method of campaigning was reminding voters that I, unlike their existing MP and now prime minister, actually lived in the constituency. On countless occasions I would see old partisan party loyalties melt away as I asked residents: 'If you or I were to fall down the stairs tonight, and need urgent medical care, which hospital would we end up in?' The answer was always the same: 'Hillingdon Hospital'. I would follow with 'Now, if Boris Johnson was to fall down the stairs tonight, where do you think he would end up?' A silence, followed by a resigned nod of acceptance, and then a whole new conversation. Our interactions were all of a sudden more intimate, less party political, and more a conversation between neighbours.

A perfect example of these sorts of conversations we were having all across the constituency was recorded by Anoosh Chakelian in the *New Statesman*:

> Milani thinks their next race for Uxbridge could be
> a poignant point in British politics. "That Portillo
> Moment I think is something that will happen,"
> he says.

A traditionally Tory outer-London seat, with Labour areas concentrated in the south, it will take over 5,000 votes to unseat Johnson.

Yet his majority was more than halved in 2017, and Milani is confident he'll win next time, predicting – like a growing number of Westminster insiders – that the next election will be this year.

So how do you topple a celebrity politician who everyone recognises?

"He's like from Hollywood, he's a character and a half, a different level!" smiles a father in sports kit who comes to the door; he has lived in Yiewsley 13 years and has Indian heritage. "Genuinely, I don't vote," he tells Milani. "They're all from Eton. The system's made for the elitists – in England and India, it's the same."

Milani explains that he's never been to Eton, and that he lived on this very road. "We need people in Westminster who know what it's like to be us."

"I'm from a working-class background," the man nods. "Poor people don't need welfare help, they need help and opportunities – to go to a club, to educate, go to an evening thing. I use the amenities here – the area is lovely, but the quality has gone, cut-backs, cut-backs, cut-backs. The hospital is horrible, they're overrun."

Coming away with a "100 per cent" promise of a vote, Milani tells me Johnson's star is falling among these residents.[1]

Yet, for all the success we found on the doorstep talking to local people about the issues their families face on a daily basis, the overall narrative of the campaign seemed to always be the same: '24-year-old Muslim immigrant looking to unseat the prime minister.'

Occasionally, I would also be reminded of this on the doorstep. In August 2019 I knocked on the door of a middle-aged couple who answered with bright beaming smiles.

'Good afternoon guys, I hope you don't mind me calling. My name is Ali Milani and I am the local Labour candidate for Uxbridge and South Ruislip in the next election. I was just going around the neighbourhood meeting local residents and speaking about some of the issues that you care most about.'

A standard opening line from me.

'Ah yes, we've had some of your leaflets come through the door' the wife replied. 'I wondered when I saw your picture, where are you from?'

'I'm from Uxbridge, just like you guys. I actually live just five minutes down the road from here.'

She wasn't convinced. 'No, I mean where are you *really* from?'

'Uxbridge. I've grown up in West London for almost all my life.' Let's give her one more chance.

'No, dear, I mean, where are you really, really from? Like ethnically?' There we go.

'I was born in Iran and both my parents are Iranian, but I, myself, have only ever known London and Britain as home.'

'Ah, I thought so when I saw your picture.' She pointed to the headshot at the front of the leaflet I had just handed her. 'Well, I'm sorry dear but we aren't going to be supporting you. We think the local MP should be actually from here, you know? Like fully English. All the best in your campaign though.'

Her racism was so polite, it disarmed me. I thanked the couple for their time and walked back to our canvassing group. I told James what had happened: 'I'm well confused, mate, she was racist, I think, but she was so nice about it.' We laughed, but it was a laugh that for both of us contained within it serious concern – how much of this was out there?

* * *

British politics has been wrestling with immigration and race for decades, but the 2010s had seen the issue explode onto the top of the agenda.

In 1997, when New Labour shot to power under the leadership of Tony Blair, only 3 per cent of the general public polled cited immigration as a key issue on their mind in the voting booth. Nearly 30 years later, as we approached the 2016 EU referendum, that figure would rise to a staggering 48 per cent. By the late 2010s immigration had become the single most important and toxic issue in British politics. More than the NHS, the housing crisis, education and global peace and security, it was immigration that was the prominent issue on the minds and lips of voters through the 2010 General Election, and through to our exit from the EU following the 2019 General Election.

In these interceding years, the landscape of our politics has radically changed. From the rise of the far-right and the introduction and prominence of UKIP and Nigel Farage, to the hostile environment, the Windrush scandal and the pictures of migrants drowning in the Mediterranean.

So what has changed?

Well, nothing. The systemic and institutional racism that has existed in our politics is as old as the state itself. This racism has always been a driving factor as it pertains to the political discourse surrounding immigration in Britain. Let's not forget, British politics has a litany of historic examples: in 1955, Winston Churchill wanted to fight a general election with the slogan 'Keep England White';[2] in 1965, Conservative MP Peter Griffiths had been elected on the slogan 'If you want a n★★★er for a neighbour, vote Labour';[3] and in 1968, Enoch Powell warned of 'rivers of blood' if non-white immigration was not put to an end.[4,5] So there has never been a time where immigration hasn't been an issue interwoven with racism and used in Westminster for cynical gain.

But it is certainly true that in more recent times, particularly from 1997 through to 2016, the prominence of immigration as a key issue rose rapidly to the forefront of the mind of the average voter. It went from an issue at the bottom of the voter priorities table – comfortably behind the NHS, housing, education and foreign affairs – to being the single biggest topic on the media airways and at the doorstep.

Traditional right-wing politicians and pundits will have a simple and lazy explanation behind the rise of immigration as a prominent issue in politics. Their claim, most often, is that under New Labour Britain opened its doors up to swathes of migrants to flood our towns and cities, taking jobs, school places and hospital appointments away from 'ordinary working people' (white – they mean white when they use this term). This, in turn, according to them, caused widespread angst among traditional populations around the country who have seen their towns and cities change too quickly, and their public services placed under too much pressure.

Their narrative for nearly three decades has been that 'sneering, out-of-touch, big-city politicians who favour foreigners and open borders are hopelessly oblivious to the struggles and the so-called "legitimate concerns" of ordinary working people'.[6] This was the very basis of one of David Cameron's main 2010 election promises, to reduce net migration figures to 'the tens of thousands rather than the hundreds of thousands'.[7]

The trouble with this analysis is that it just does not stand up to the most basic scrutiny. From the New Labour government of 1997 to the Conservative-Liberal Democrat coalition of 2010, the UK's laws on, and treatment of, migrants has been as strict as at any time in modern politics.

Look at the record. In 1997, Britain had approximately 32,500 overall asylum claims made to the Home Office, of which 81 per cent were refused.[8] In 1999, the Immigration and Asylum Act was passed under a Labour administration and 'formalised the use of detention centres as a routine administrative measure rather than an exception'. The Act 'also replaced cash benefits for asylum seekers with vouchers, since cash benefits were, in the words of Labour's Home Secretary Jack Straw, "a major pull factor that encourage fraudulent claims"'.[9,10]

Later, in 2001, then Labour Home Secretary David Blunkett would go on to tout the idea of forcing asylum-seekers to carry national identity cards,[11] and proposed teaching asylum-seeker children in separate classrooms as local schools were being 'swamped' by non-English-speaking migrants.[12] This was an outrageous idea that would be scrapped quite quickly as a result of the backlash it created all across the country.

This baton was then picked up by a Conservative-led coalition and ran further, as they would introduce arbitrary targets on net migration figures in an effort to drive down the number of people entering the country, and passed new Immigration Acts in 2014 and 2016 'which included myriad measures to prevent people from accessing employment, healthcare, housing, education, banking and other basic services'.[13] A poignant moment that provides a unique insight into the perspectives of this government would be David Cameron's choice of words when describing Jeremy Corbyn's decision to meet refugees in Calais. The prime minister derided the Labour leader for meeting 'a bunch of migrants'.[14]

So this claim that, for 20 years, successive British governments have opened the door and laid out the red carpet for migrants is simply not true. It might be politically convenient, but it is not based on reality. Yes, net migration increased over the 1997–2016 period, but there has been, both in words and deeds, a seriously hostile environment surrounding migrants and refugees for most of this period.

Something else did change in this time. It struck at the end of 2007 and through the beginning of 2008: the global financial crisis.

The global financial crisis – commonly referred to as the 2008 crash – sparked a global recession unlike any other since the Second World War. Following years of predatory lending, targeting of low-income families by banks, and reckless gambling by financial institutions, the entire sector came tumbling down and witnessed the bankruptcy of one of the world's oldest financial services firm – Lehman Brothers.

In the span of a few months, the crisis crippled the global economy and saw a loss of more than US$2 trillion from the global economy.[15] In the US alone, US$3.4 trillion was lost in real estate wealth, US$7.4 trillion in stock exchange wealth and approximately US$5,800 in lost income for each household.[16] In the UK the recession was equally painful. The downturn in the economy was greater than any other since the Great Depression of the 1930s. Professor John Van Reenen, Director of the ESRC-funded Centre for Economic Performance at the London School of Economics and Political Science, said: 'Since the crisis broke we have suffered a period of depressed national income that has lasted for even longer than in the inter-war period. Poor growth is the number one economic problem facing Britain today.'[17]

It was not just a financial crisis, or even a global economic disaster, but a crisis for capitalism as a whole.

Naturally, most people expected repercussions – for those responsible for gambling away our economy and causing so much pain and suffering to be held accountable. For there to be justice. But instead, something else happened. Something weird.

In the years that followed the crisis, there seemed to be a collective cognitive dissonance in our politics as to why the crisis had taken place and who was to blame. Rather than recognising that a reckless and unregulated banking sector was always going to lead us to the edge of oblivion, the political conversation became about how too much government spending was to blame. As opposed to coming down on the financiers who walked away with millions in bonuses as the rest of us lost our jobs, houses and livelihoods, attention was turned to the immigrants and refugees, who were suddenly to blame for the strain on public services.

As a new Conservative government came into power, the entire crisis was rebranded. The roll-out of austerity measures by David Cameron and George Osborne was accompanied by a new narrative that erased all the crimes and misdemeanours of the banking sector, and placed the burden on the public and the most vulnerable among us. To quote Mark Baum from the film *The Big Short*:

> I have a feeling in a few years people are going to be
> doing what they always do when the economy tanks.
> They will be blaming immigrants and poor people.

All of this happened with very little resistance from the Labour Party or senior Labour politicians. I don't know if they felt they couldn't overturn the narrative, whether they actually agreed with it, or were just too scared to tackle the topic, but in the 2010s it became the norm across political parties to speak of overspending by government and 'controls on immigration' as a method of relieving the pressure on our schools, hospitals and public services.

As the grip of austerity tightened on communities all across the UK, people began looking around them for something to blame. And the message from Westminster was unchallenged: it was the last Labour government and the black and brown families next door. It was highlighted by Danny Dorling, Professor of Geography at the University of Oxford when writing for the *British Medical Journal*: 'almost all other European countries tax more effectively, spend more on health, and do not tolerate our degree of economic inequality. To distract us from these national failings, we have been encouraged to blame immigration and the EU.'[18]

So for years, as people sat for hours in local hospitals waiting for treatment, they didn't see the underfunding of nurses and doctors – they saw the fellow patient in the waiting room who looked different to them. As they struggled to get their kids into a good local school, they didn't see the chronic mismanagement of state schools – they saw the kids who did get in looking different to their own. A narrative unchallenged by politicians in the public discourse becomes fact, and it was now fact that the tough times we were in were the fault of immigrants, whether they were coming from Eastern Europe or beyond.

There was a fear in the Labour Party, then and now, to even tackle the issue of immigration. No one in mainstream political discourse was making the positive case for immigration, defending the most vulnerable in our society and pushing back against the patent lies coming from the right. This was admitted as much by a senior adviser of former Labour leader Ed Miliband: 'We spent five years being shit-scared', he said. 'If we had the time again, I would force Ed to do a speech on the fallacy of blaming immigration for the reality of austerity cuts.'[19]

But it was too late – the scene had been set. I recall one of the key moments that it became clear to me. It was in the 2015 General Election, as Ed Miliband participated in a *Question Time* town hall-style debate where he took questions from the audience. He was asked whether he would admit that the last Labour government had spent too much. Ed answered instinctually: 'No, I don't, and I know you may not agree with that.'[20] The audience gasped and the air left the room. They could not believe the answer.

What is remarkable about that moment is that Ed Miliband was absolutely right. Not only had the spending of the last Labour government not been too much, but it also had absolutely nothing to do with the economic crash that had led to the woes of our country. But it was too late. The narrative had been set over years where Labour had gone along with the rebranding of the 2008 crisis and not challenged the mainstream discourse. And the same was true on the question of immigration. It was too late.

By the time I had shot to prominence in 2019, the scene had already been set. That is why there was such an obsession with my being a 'young immigrant' taking on Boris Johnson. It is also why, despite my personal frustrations with being branded as just that one thing, we did not run from it. I wanted our story to make the positive case. I wanted it to be possible, in the eyes of every young person in Uxbridge and South Ruislip and across the country watching, whose story resembles mine, for a person like me to beat someone like Boris Johnson. If a young, Muslim, immigrant can make history and defeat a sitting prime minister, then all things are possible.

It has always been my belief that one of the most important traits of a political leader is courage. It is not our job to just tell voters what we think they want to hear, or what has been determined as popular in some basement focus group, but rather what we think is right, what will improve the lives of our community. Sometimes, this means turning something unpopular into something that is popular. It means making the case for something you believe in. This is not only real political courage, but also the sign of a talented leader. And on the issue of immigration, we lacked that for decades.

We were paralysed by fear, scared stiff by the results of focus groups. No one had the courage to come out, make the case and change minds. Our story and our campaign wouldn't change that on its own, but it could help. It was a start.

★ ★ ★

The discourse around race in Britain requires the same political courage as the question of immigration, the same willingness to radically change the nature of the debate.

Racism has always been a reality in my own life, long before any of my political campaigns. In the earlier parts of my journey I felt it, but I did not really see it. The institutional racism that lived with us in our education system, in policing, and even in the housing system was as part of daily life as anything else. Things we believed were normal were anything but normal outside our communities. The incessant and racist 'stop and search' method of policing that only ever sowed mistrust between the police and us. The attainment gap that saw non-white students 20 per cent less likely to get top grades compared to our white colleagues. The roll-out of the Prevent strategy that instilled fear into any Muslim student who might Google the wrong thing and end being interrogated about their motives and religious beliefs.

But as a young man in one of London's most diverse communities, I was rarely conscious of how alive racism was in our society. Because, when I was stopped by the same police officers three times in the same week, so were my other classmates in school. When my mum had her income halted by the local authority because her English wasn't good enough in a job centre interview, my friends had told me the same stories in their households.

My own experience with racism in Britain largely pertains to the rapid rise in and normalisation of Islamophobia – both in politics and in society.

Islamophobia in today's modern Britain represents one of the most mainstream forms of racism that exists. Since the 2016 EU referendum, we have seen a sharp rise in hate crime and in particular, a rise in violent and non-violent Islamophobic attacks. Home Office figures released in October 2020 showed that of all the recorded hate crime offences committed in England and Wales, the highest percentage of attacks was perpetrated against Muslims. Of the 6,822 religiously motivated hate crimes recorded by the police in 2019/20, over 50 per cent were targeted towards Muslims.[21]

Reports on social mobility and economic disparities have also consistently shown that Muslims often face Islamophobia in the workforce. Muslim women in particular, who face the most intense elements of Islamophobia in the UK, are the most economically disadvantaged group, with the highest level of unemployment compared to other religious and ethnic groups in the country.

So, while there is some debate within the Muslim community about its exact nature and the particular language used to define it, the existence of Islamophobia as a form of racism is undenied. The APPG (All-Party Parliamentary Group) on British Muslims published a report in 2018 introducing the first working definition of Islamophobia. Following two years of consultation across the Muslim community, the political sphere, charities and other relevant organisations, the definition was agreed and passed:

> Islamophobia is rooted in racism and is a type of racism that targets expressions of Muslimness or perceived Muslimness.[22]

> Contemporary examples of Islamophobia in public life, the media, schools, the workplace, and in encounters between religions and non-religions in the public sphere could, taking into account the overall context, include, but are not limited to: "causing, calling for, aiding or justifying acts of aggression against Muslims"; "dehumanising, demonising or making stereotypical allegations about Muslims" and "prescribing to/propagating conspiracy theories about Muslims."[23]

The APPG understood, as most Muslims do, the racialised form Islamophobia most often presents in our society. When Mohammed Saleem, an 82-year-old father and grandfather, was fatally stabbed on his way home in Birmingham, the perpetrators did not ask him to recite his testament of faith before their attack. When Muslim women are attacked on buses, and trains, and on our streets, attackers don't stop for a discussion on which theological school of thought they belong to; they do it because of how they look.

Yet despite all the evidence, the testimony of lived experience from Muslim communities and the data proving its prominence in our society, Islamophobia remains one of the few forms of racism where its very existence is denied – from both conservative and liberal voices. In fact, the Conservative Party has, to date, refused to adopt the APPG definition, even with the scathing criticisms from within and without their party, including by former Tory chair Baroness Warsi.

The arguments that every Muslim has to put up with are neither imaginative nor particularly coherent: (1) Islam is not a race, and therefore Islamophobia cannot be a form of racism; (2) Islamophobia is a term that's use by a secret cabal of Islamists who are trying to shut down theological criticisms of a religion; or even (3) Islamophobic racism cannot exist against Muslims as Muslims are often from different races.

Painfully, these arguments are not confined to far-right rallies or the dark sections of the web; they are mainstream.

In 2019 Trevor Phillips wrote an article for *The Spectator* titled 'The notion of "Islamophobia" is being used to stifle honest debate.'[24] Mr Phillips, a broadcaster, writer and member of the Labour Party, argued that what is being demanded by representative groups such as the Muslim Council of Britain is 'a kind of media apartheid, under which Muslim communities are reported on according to rules and conventions not applied to others; where work by non-Muslim professionals is judged by different standards from those who claim to follow the faith.'[25] To this day, despite long-standing complaints from Muslim organisations and members, Trevor Phillips remains a member of the party.

Melanie Phillips, another mainstream political commentator, wrote an article for *The Times* titled 'Islamophobia is a fiction to shut down debate', and argued that 'there was no equivalence between anti-Semitism and Islamophobia. The former was a deranged demonisation of a people; the latter was used to shut down debate.'[26]

So, despite the overwhelming evidence of institutional Islamophobia in the media (discussed in Chapter 4), the data showing a rapid rise in violent and non-violent attacks, and the avalanche of Muslim voices citing a culture of racism in our politics and society, those such as Trevor Phillips and Melanie Phillips, those on both the right and some on the left, continue to deny the very existence of the kind of racism people like me have felt and continue to live with.

The fight for us isn't just one to eradicate racism, but to have it simply recognised as a reality.

★ ★ ★

Islamophobia, as a form of racism, is certainly not a new concept. It has been around for hundreds of years. In the 18th, 19th and early 20th century, the first significant wave of Muslim immigrants arrived in the UK, to work in manual labour, farming and on the docks. They settled and formed communities in Cardiff, Liverpool and London. Since these earliest of days, with the settlement of the new Muslims, Islamophobia has existed in our society, from orientalist views of the Middle East and Muslims as backward and unevolved peoples, to perceived threats to 'Western ways of life'. But there was one event that changed everything, from the scale of Islamophobia to its intensity in the public discourse.

I don't remember 9/11.

My mother tells me she does. She recalls watching the towers fall on the screen of a small TV at a local gym. Rows of people on a pavement outside, transfixed by the small screens, watching what looked like scenes from a Hollywood film come to life. Some shed tears; others were suspended in disbelief, watching the tragedy unfold.

I do, however, remember 7/7 quite vividly. It was a Thursday morning. I had pulled a sickie from school on that particular Thursday morning, pretending I was unwell, determined to stay home to watch Dick van Dyke's *Diagnosis: Murder* on TV. Pulling sickies on my mum was notoriously difficult in our house. She would always insist my sister and I were well enough and should go to school. But on this occasion, remarkably, and without much debate, she let me stay in bed.

The calls starting coming in a little while after 9am. I was the only one in the living room as our phone began ringing incessantly. Family from abroad, friends from the UK – it seemed like everyone we knew. Finally, my grandmother got through from the US to ask if we were all safe. I was confused – the panic in her voice frightened me even before I knew what was happening. As I passed the phone to my mother, I switched on the TV and saw the coverage – the images of a London bus mangled almost beyond recognition, the shots of commuters covered in blood and soot. At 10 years old, I, like my mum four years prior, was frozen to the screen. It was the most afraid I had ever been.

Then it got very real, very fast. In the midst of the reporting, I recognised where one of the attacks had taken place: Edgware Road Station. Edgware Road is one of London's busiest areas, just a stone's throw away from central tourist hotspots and the shopping districts of our city. It was also the closest station to our school, and my sister had gone to school that morning. The atmosphere of national tragedy quickly shifted in our little flat to personal panic.

Our city changed that day. Our world changed.

My life, and the lives of all the little boys and girls like me, had changed irreversibly. I knew it when I went back into school following the attacks – the comments thrown at the Muslim kids in our class. 'Terrorist', 'Suicide bomber', 'Where is Osama?' It wasn't just our school or even just in schools; it was everywhere.

Leonie Jackson, in *Islamophobia in Britain*, recalls the immediate fallout of the attacks among her university undergraduate politics cohort:

> As we meandered in the classroom, waiting for the instructor to arrive, a new polarisation formed among the class. The hijackings were on everyone's lips, and in the heated conversations several people turned to Sofia to explain them. She was Muslim, and so, the media loudly exclaimed, were the hijackers. In unease and confusion students looked to her for an explanation. What was it about Islam that had driven these attacks? Did she think the hijackers were right? Did all Muslims secretly share these grudges? As she tried to deal with the increasingly hostile questioning, one woman turned to me, shaking her head disapprovingly, and muttered "how can she say this has nothing to do with Islam? This is all about Islam."[27]

Muslims were the enemy now, and whether it was comments made in our classrooms being unchallenged, or political narratives being drawn up in Westminster and on TV, there was no doubt that for the foreseeable future the lives of millions of Muslims would be faced with either a quiet suspicion or palpable hostility. As highlighted by Milly Williamson and Gholam Khiabany, all of this has created 'a false cultural binary of "us" and "them"' and also placed Muslim women as central to 'the debate on modernity, culture and politics'.[28]

Islamophobia, for me, had become part of my daily experience as a candidate.

In the early part of the primary race to be the Labour candidate, I had it thrown at me from Labour members. There were small instances, such as members claiming at a local meeting that 'Ali just isn't one of us', despite me having been a local and active member for more than five years. And there were bigger instances, such as a local member ringing me up on the phone and asking 'if I supported terrorists', if I, myself, 'was a terrorist', and if 'Muslims could even be MPs', given our propensity, as this particular member put it, to 'support violence'. Many of these cases were reported to the party's complaints procedure, but no action was ever taken. In fact, in the case of the latter example, I submitted a complaint in September 2018 and the first I heard back from the Labour complaints department was 13 months later, in October 2019, to ask me to resubmit my complaint as it had been lost by a staff member.

Later on, in the autumn of 2019, at the peak of our campaign and as our race was the most talked about election campaign, I remember a particularly uncomfortable conversation with a Labour staffer who suggested that I may want to sanitise my name on the ballot from 'Ali Reza Milani' to just 'Ali Milani' to help make it 'easier for voters to support me'. Make it less Muslim, is what they meant. I remember laughing at the suggestion and simply replying that, given my opponent's name was 'Alexander Boris de Pfeffel Johnson', I didn't think I was the one with the unusual sounding name.

My own experience in a short time had left me in no doubt – Islamophobia in the Labour Party was a very serious problem. It wasn't just that I had experienced it from members – this was a form of racism that existed throughout British society, and so its existence in some form in Labour was to be expected. It was rather the manner in which the party dealt with complaints and incidences. The lack of urgency from party officials, the disinterest in tackling it as a serious issue and the lack of any real structural mechanisms to deal with this, and other forms of racism, was alarming.

Research conducted by the Labour Muslim Network – based on the largest consultation of Muslim members in history – proved that the situation was even more dire than my earlier suspicions. The report published found that over one in four Muslim members and supporters of Labour had experienced Islamophobia within the party. Nearly half of the members did not believe that the party took the issue of Islamophobia seriously, and more than half did not 'trust the leadership of the party to tackle Islamophobia effectively'.

None of this was particularly surprising to me. I had seen it and felt it throughout my candidacy. While Labour had been quick to criticise the Conservatives on their record on Islamophobia (which is a plenty-long charge sheet), it was our responsibility to get our own house in order first, to lead by example.

And while the vast majority of members on the ground had been the most inspiring and supportive groups of people I had ever encountered, it was the structures of the party that I had struggled with.

The truth is that the Labour Party has a problem with Islamophobia – its prevalence, its denial by some and our inability, so far, to tackle it. But I believe we can. Not because I have had a shortage of Islamophobic experiences in the party – I sure haven't – but because of the people I have met along the journey. As our campaign reached national notoriety and fame, our campaign sessions had been full of volunteers. Hundreds of members from across the country would flock to Uxbridge and South Ruislip to support our campaign. All from different ethnicities, ages, regions and life backgrounds. I saw in them, every day, a belief in a Labour Party that would root out racism from its own ranks, a party that would defeat racism in British society as whole.

The Labour Party is not just its leader. It's not just its general secretary. It's certainly not just its MPs. Sorry, I know that it must be stinging for some of you to hear that. It is those faces, those people who give up their evenings, their holidays, their time with their family and their kids to fight for a better world. They are the real Labour Party.

★ ★ ★

Outside Labour, it was the tightening of the betting odds that set off the biggest wave of racist hate mail and threats. I had never gambled in my life, but as it turns out, gambling companies also set odds for political races. Through the summer to the autumn of 2019, bookies had slashed our odds of beating Boris in Uxbridge and South Ruislip from around 33/1 to 6/1. After a lot of explaining from James and Andy from our team, I quickly learned that this was something called 'shortening'. It meant that betting companies saw our odds of winning as much more likely than they had done just a few months ago.

As this was picked up, the propensity and frequency of the Islamophobia we had to deal with hit its highest peak. It mostly came through social media, some through written mail and occasionally face to face – either at a campaign event or while I was out and about in Uxbridge. Facebook groups began surging with a plethora of horrendously racist comments from all around the country:

NO NO NO SEND HIM BACK FOR GODS SAKE.

Why don't we just invite all of the far eastern world to stand.

Look out Uxbridge or is it Muslibridge now?

Why do these lot think we should bow and scrap to them. Who the hell do they think they are. Take note they came to the UK to be looked after, one parent family mother spoke very little English and now he wants to try and run our country. To many of these bloody lot in this country.

They [meaning us] couldn't run a bath let alone a country, look at the state of Londonistan, we will

have it back though, very very soon everyone got
their yellow vests.

I blamed Boris Johnson for much of the abuse I was receiving.
Not because he was in any way directly involved – he wasn't – but
he had been one of the actors guilty of introducing this divisive
form of politics into our mainstream national conversation. His
history of using offensive, often racist, language for political
expediency was a long one. And I was dealing with the fallout
of the kind of politics he, and those like him, had introduced.

Boris had a history of using terms such as 'flag-waving
piccaninnies' and had referred to African people as having
'watermelon smiles',[29] he has likened Muslim women who
wear burqas to 'letterboxes' and 'bank robbers',[30] and he wrote
for *The Spectator* that 'to any non-Muslim reader of the Koran,
Islamophobia – fear of Islam – seems a natural reaction and,
indeed, exactly what that text is intended to provoke'.[31]

You might think this a result of Boris Johnson's buffoon-like
attitude. Here's a guy who speaks first, and thinks second. But
having gotten to know him, his office, and those around him
in the intensity of this campaign, I knew it was more. Boris was
not a stumbling idiot; he was calculating. In my view, his use
of right-wing, divisive, sometimes racist language and imagery
was a carefully thought-out attempt to win favour among the
far-right in Britain, to slowly gather himself an electoral base.
The success of the Trump project in the US would surely have
only emboldened that project.

He wasn't alone in employing this form of politics. Zack
Goldsmith had been widely criticised for using similar tactics in
his unsuccessful mayoral race against Sadiq Khan. Just like the
issue of immigration, mainstream politicians like Boris and Zack
were using distraction tactics to win support. As argued by Tahir
Abbas, this is a kind of politics that is 'guilty of normalising
anti-immigrant and anti-Muslim sentiment due to its inability to
alleviate these social concerns through binding legislation, thus
giving credence to elements of the far right who feel justified in
subscribing to the view that Muslims en masse are a problem'.[32]

Tahir Abbas concludes that 'a virulent strain of Islamophobic,
xenophobic and exclusivist ethnic nationalism is taking hold

in England, with significant risks for community relations and national politics, all of which are continuities of racism reinvented in an age of anger, fear and loathing centred on Islam and Muslims in post-normal times'.[33] This anger and fear was what I was feeling in the messages of hate, and the threats on my life, which were now headed my way at an alarming rate.

Ultimately, the campaign launch went off without a hitch. Over 300 supporters gathered on the steps of Hillingdon Civic Centre in an unbelievable show of support. The threat on this occasion didn't materialise. But as I delivered my stump speech, half scanning the crowd for a potential attack, I remember noticing their faces – the diversity – in race, age, religion – in everything. As they nodded, and smiled, and cheered, and laughed, I knew that this form of political courage was easier than had been made out by some politicians.

We just had to flip the image. To show the country and not me on the stump, the crowd I could see when I stood up to speak. This was the real story of Britain. These were the real faces of Britain. These people better resembled the lives of ordinary people than the halls of Eton or Westminster. All these people, who had come from near and far, in the hope of a better world. It was them we had to show. It wouldn't be enough to dismantle racism and anti-migrant bigotry in the country. That would take the dismantlement of centuries of policies and norms, and ideas beyond this book and my own story. But in their faces, I saw people willing to try. And that was enough for me.

6

'Running while broke'

No one ever forgets the first time they saw their parents cry.

For me, it was one of my earliest and most vivid memories, and it is something that to this day is painful to recall. At the age of 10 or 11 I would often spend my weekends at the back of our West London council estate. In the absence of video games at home or cable and satellite TV, children in our neighbourhood would often find themselves passing endless hours in parks and on the local estates.

On this particular day, I remember stumbling back home after hours of playing football, and being told off by neighbours and shopkeepers, to see if dinner was ready. It was a usual routine for all of us on the estate to break for a combined lunch and dinner, and to meet back in the evening to resume whatever particular activity we had come up with that day. My family lived in a small flat held together by one long corridor that ran right down the middle and connected three rooms. To your immediate right was the kitchen, and this was the first room you encountered on entering the flat. Further down there was one room to the left, which was my mum's room, and one room straight ahead, shared by my sister and I. Today, that flat would probably seem a claustrophobic nightmare to me, but back then, it felt like a castle.

On this particular evening, I came home to find my mum hunched over an electric rice cooker, trying to hide her tears. Frustratedly wrestling with the machine, it was quickly evident that something was seriously wrong – mum never allowed us to see signs of her struggling or her pain. In one singular moment, all the energy and adrenaline of the games and adventures I had been part of that day drained from me. This was not right, and I knew it. Quickly retreating into my bedroom, I began to ask my sister what had happened to upset mum so badly. My sister, who herself was quite emotional, told me the story: our mum had not been able to afford to pay for both the gas and electricity meter this week. Having to choose between the gas and electricity meter, she had opted to keep the lights on, as she believed it would be less obvious to us of the financial struggles we were in. But this also meant that the gas stove would not work to cook dinner, and so she had been forced to use the electric rice cooker to make dinner for us that evening. This was a stinging reminder to her, in that moment, of the daily struggle that was the simple act of feeding her kids.

This memory has haunted me for most of my life. It's a picture of a working-class, single mother doing all she could to provide, but still not able to make ends meet. It is an image that encompasses the pain, poverty and inequality woven into the very fabric of one of the richest countries on the planet. This moment had a profound impact on my life and outlook on the world, because I have since come to understand the constant pain my mum must have been experiencing – the struggle of not knowing where our next meal was going to come from, the anxiety over every outstanding bill and the heartache of not being able to offer her children the luxuries she saw others take for granted every day. This memory also hurts because I know it is not mine alone; it is the story of millions of families across the country, millions of single parents who have all shed the same tears my mum did that evening.

When I was young, that pain and those tears were not something I, or those around me, were particularly aware of. We lived in the wonderfully engrossing ignorance of infancy. For our friends, family and community, our stories were all the same, and so the challenges and barriers in our way weren't to the forefront of our conscious mind. We didn't see them. But as I grew up and became alert to my circumstances, it became impossible to deny that money and our financial circumstances had had an immeasurable impact on both the opportunities afforded to me and also my confidence in seeking them out. From the schools I was able to attend to the friends I made throughout my childhood and adolescence, from the work experience I was offered and participated in to the networks and circles I had access to – every part of my youth and adolescence was influenced by my family's class and our financial limitations.

This was as true – if not more so – later on in my story, both as a candidate and political activist.

More than any other variable, it is money that most influences the type of politicians that end up in Westminster. At both an individual and institutional level, there is no more decisive a factor than the financial circumstances of politicians and political parties. I know this to be true, because it is perhaps the most significant aspect of my own story. Although I grew up in relative poverty for all my young life, it was only once I became a parliamentary candidate and a political figure in British politics that I truly felt held back by my own financial insecurities. For all the luck, circumstance and privilege I have been afforded in my political and personal journey, there is one thing that has always been impossible to deny: money has been the emphatic factor in my life.

★ ★ ★

We all know how important money is in politics, but what we don't often appreciate is how decisive it is in political campaigns. Our campaign had completely changed since its first laps in the autumn of 2018. We were no longer just running a campaign against one of British politics' biggest celebrities; we were now attempting to defeat a sitting prime minister, a feat never before accomplished. That goal and my journey gave me a unique view of the real role of money in our politics; I got to witness first hand the true scale of influence that exists behind the scenes. It was confirmation of all I had suspected and known; like opening a watch and looking deep into its mechanics, I could see with complete clarity an undeniable truth, that our democracy is too often dictated by those with the deepest pockets and the largest wallets.

The influence of money in British politics can broadly be split into two categories: big money and small money – big money being the vice-like grip of multinational corporations and their billionaire owners on our political institutions and organisations, and small money being the impact of personal and familial wealth and class at an individual level in politics. Both are critically influential, and both set the scene for the vast majority of our current political actors.

* * *

The influence and control of big money on British politics goes back to the dawn of democracy on these islands. For as long as there have been elections and parliaments, the richest in society have attempted to buy power. In fact, before our so-called 'modern political system', it was only the very wealthy and landowners who got a vote and a say on who would go on to govern in Westminster. One of the earliest attempts to rid the political system of the total domination by the rich and powerful was the Representation of the People Act in 1832. Also known as the First Reform Act or the Great Reform Act, it was a hugely influential piece of legislation in the history of the British electoral system. The Act brought about significant change to the electoral system that, among other things, introduced representation for cities, gave small landowners, tenant farmers, shopkeepers and householders (paying a yearly rent of £10 or more) the right to vote, and created 67 new constituencies.

Marshalled by the then Prime Minister Charles Grey, of the Whig Party, the legislation was created 'for correcting divers abuses that [had] long prevailed in the choice of members to serve in the [House of Commons]'.[1] Prior to this legislation, most MPs nominally represented boroughs, as opposed to the constituencies we know of today. Due to the number of electors being quite small and varied in many places, the selection of MPs was frequently controlled by one very powerful patron. An example of this would be Charles Howard, 11th Duke of Norfolk, who controlled the selection of MPs in over 11 different boroughs.

Another salient historic example of complete financial dominance in local British politics is the Sandwich constituency by-election in 1880, a personal favourite of mine.

When one of the sitting liberal MPs accepted a peerage in 1880, the local constituency was thrown into a by-election that quickly turned into a rambunctious affair. In a battle between the Conservatives and the Liberals, the contest very quickly descended into extensive 'treating' of electors (often with free food and drink) and the downright bribery of voters with 'heavy bag[s] of gold' brought up from London.[2] As evidence of bribery and corruption mounted, a Royal Commission was appointed to investigate. In the end it was found that of the 2,115 electors in the constituency, 1,850 had voted, 900 of whom admitted that they had been bribed and a further 100 admitted to bribing others. The results of the report were so damning that the constituency of Sandwich had to be abolished altogether and incorporated into the Eastern Kent county division. Imagine that, an election campaign so corrupt, that they had to abolish the whole constituency.

Now, much has changed since the early 1800s. One can reasonably expect to live beyond the lofty ages of 30 to 40, we no longer send people to American and Australian colonies for relatively minor criminal offences, and I don't need to take a walk through my garden and front lawn to use a functioning bathroom. Despite this undeniable progress in some areas of life, however, I am not sure the same can be said about the influence of wealth and capital on our politics and our parliamentary systems.

★ ★ ★

As the Conservative Party's leadership election began, we knew we were in big trouble. Boris Johnson would be a prime minister with the smallest majority in his own constituency for decades. The entire political world knew that a general election was beckoning, and that once Boris was crowned Tory leader and the country's prime minister, there was no way this now marginal seat wasn't going to be flooded with big money. We had to fight back, or at least try, or we were about to be blown away by the Number 10 machine.

James Robertson – who had become my communications guru and adviser by this point – suggested we launch a public fundraiser on the day of Boris's coronation. He pointed out that people all around the country would be watching on as a new prime minister was elected, and would feel helpless having played no part in that election. As a new leader was being chosen and only Tory members would be getting a vote, as sure as anything, there would be thousands of people looking for a way to fight back: our campaign could give them a place to point that energy and fight.

Scrambling for time, our team organised an online fundraiser, wrote emails and letters to be sent out to supporters, and James and I began working on a campaign video to launch. Without the money within the campaign to pay for a professional campaign video, and my personal finances having been stretched too far already, we found someone who believed in our campaign and offered to shoot the video without immediate payment. Frances Freeman is a supremely talented, independent videographer who agreed to help us develop the video and who would only take payment if we hit our fundraising goal.

With Frances on board, James writing our script and the rest of our team working on a fundraising strategy, I was feverish at the very idea of having some level of financial freedom for our campaign. In all other aspects of this election, I had felt in control. I knew my story, our ideas and my ability to communicate our message would overcome all other barriers. But when it came to money, I felt hopeless.

In the space of two weeks we had developed an emotional and clear campaign video, an online fundraiser people could contribute to, and a clear understanding of where their money was going. We chose not to accept any donations over £500 and, as per Electoral Commission rules, all of our donors would be UK residents. The video, which launched on the day of the Tory leadership election results, was the story of our campaign, the essence of why I was running:

> people like me aren't meant to go into politics. I wasn't born into a rich and powerful family. I grew up in a household where we had to choose between putting gas on the meter or food on our plates. We've got an opportunity to make history and banish Boris. He's got his billionaire backers, all we've got is each other.[3]

As soon as we launched the campaign and video, it went viral. I could see that where people had felt hopeless at an electoral system that would allow a few thousand Conservative members to pick the leader of the country, in our campaign they found a route to change. Labour voters, Liberals, Greens, non-voters and even disaffected Tories all contributed. In just two weeks, we had hit our target of raising £5,000. As one donor put it, 'Go Ali. I have never donated to a political party or campaign before. I will actually vote LibDem but ... recognising the possibility of unseating Boris having such a positive effect on British Politics, I could not help but get involved ... sorry I can't help in person but I live a long way away. ... You know the B will do everything and anything ... best of luck.' Another simply said 'Get the lying shit out'.[4]

Both very good points well made.

Overwhelmed by the response, I was buoyed up to get out and do everything I could. People were counting on us and we could not let them down. Our average donation was £18, and while that may not seem like much in the grand scheme of such a high-profile campaign, I knew better than most how important that could be for a single family. I knew that we had to do these donations justice.

Our new finances brought new opportunities. We could develop new leaflets that addressed the fact that our opponent was now the prime minister and residents could make history by unseating him. We could book spaces and organise community outreach events and speak directly to residents. There was so much we could do now.

Then, one Monday afternoon, we all came crashing back down to earth. As I was working through our campaign schedule for the week, I heard the familiar clang of my letterbox. As I walked to pick up the mail, I saw a big blue leaflet with Boris Johnson splashed across the front. Quickly jumping into my WhatsApp groups, I asked the rest of our team if they had also received the leaflet. It turned out that they had – every last one of them. The Johnson team had just delivered tens of thousands of leaflets, by what must have been courier, to every door in the constituency, a move that would have cost well in excess of the £5,000 we had just raised. So what had taken us a month to organise and raise, Boris Johnson and his billionaire backers had spent on one single Monday afternoon.

I knew then that there was no way we could compete with his money. This election really did have to become people vs money.

★ ★ ★

The dominance of 'big money' in politics is often dismissed in Britain as an exclusively 'American' problem. UK political analysts look across the Atlantic and compare the eye-watering amounts of money spent by lobbyist and special interest groups, and conclude that the UK is nowhere near those levels of control and influence. And who could blame them? In 2020 alone, the total spend by lobbyists in the US amounted to over US$3.49 billion[5] – more than the GDP of Guyana. David and Charles Koch, of Koch Industries, and two of the most notorious political lobbyists in the US, donated nearly US$2 billion to the Republican Party and right-wing political causes until David's death in 2019. Robert Mercer, the billionaire CEO of the hedge fund Renaissance Technologies, and key donor to Donald Trump, has himself donated over US$15.5 million[6] to a right-wing super-political action group (PAC) named 'Make America Number 1'.

So, when comparing the present situation in Westminster to those staggering figures in Washington, New York and beyond, it would be easy to simply turn the page, breathe a sigh of relief and be thankful that our politics and politicians have thus far avoided this sort of financial flooding by special interests groups and multinational corporations.

But even a mere glance beneath the rug of our politics shows that 'big money' is not just an 'American' problem; it is very much a British problem too.

If you don't believe me, just look at the Brexit referendum campaign – a cacophony of huge financial injections, foreign donors, digital misinformation and a campaign that all sides called 'broken' – that is, before the results came out. Peter Geoghegan, in *Democracy for sale: Dark money and dirty politics*, highlights a particular Democratic Unionist Party (DUP) advertising blitz as a symbolic example of the roots of the financial improprieties of the Brexit referendum. He points to one particular DUP Leave advertising programme that was bankrolled by the biggest donation in Northern Irish political history. The donation was 'routed through a secretive Scottish group' and 'linked to a former head of Saudi Arabian intelligence'.[7] Peter also goes on to highlight that the trail of money in the Brexit referendum continues 'stretching far beyond Britain's shores – from Cambridge Analytica, Steve Bannon and leading figures in Donald Trump's America to Matteo Salvini, Viktor Orbán and Europe's insurgent far right. There were corporate-funded think tanks and lobbyists with access to the highest levels of government and networks of keyboard warriors in suburban bedrooms churning out hyper-partisan news stories that spread like wildfire.'[8]

This increasing influence of 'big money', be it in campaign finance or lobbyists' culture, is undeniably a very British problem, and one that is growing at an alarming rate. While UK politics has obviously never been immune to financial impropriety and corruption, there is mounting attestation of an 'Americanisation' in the way 'big money' influences our political parties and politicians, both in scale and in nature. It is true that in raw numbers, the amounts spent are still in no way comparable between the US and UK, but the worry for progressives on this side of the Atlantic should be that here, in the UK, influence is cheaper, easier and has far fewer rules.

★ ★ ★

> We all know how it works. The lunches, the hospitality, the quiet word in your ear, the ex-ministers and ex-advisers for hire, helping big business find the right way to get its way.[9]

These were the words of former Conservative Prime Minister David Cameron in 2010, speaking before a crowd on 'rebuilding trust in politics'. So if this is how it works, and we all know this is how it works, how come nothing can be done about it?

The answer can be found in David Cameron's own story, just a little bit further down the road.

In the early 2010s, a then young and buoyant prime minister David Cameron brought an Australian banker named Alexander 'Lex' Greensill to Downing Street to work as an unpaid adviser to the Conservative administration.[10] While working for the prime minister as a 'senior adviser', the exact relationship between Lex Greensill and David Cameron remains a mystery, although business cards and reports from that time place Greensill at the heart of Number 10 during Cameron's premiership.[11]

One Brexit referendum defeat later and a resignation from Cameron as prime minister, he very quickly went on to advocate for Greensill Capital, a financial services company founded by the same former adviser Lex Greensill. In 2021 the former prime minister and his Australian banker friend were both thrown into a national lobbying scandal as it was revealed that Mr Cameron had used personal connections with senior government ministers to persistently lobby for access to a government-backed COVID-19 loan scheme for Greensill Capital. This would have allowed Greensill to issue millions of pounds worth of loans, insured by the government, to firms and businesses throughout the pandemic. While both Cameron and Greensill were unsuccessful in their attempts – and Greensill Capital has since collapsed, resulting in the loss of 440 jobs – Cameron came under intense scrutiny for allegedly exploiting personal contacts with former government colleagues for his own benefit.[12] Some news outlets reported that Cameron himself was set to make in the region of £60 million from a potential deal, an accusation he branded as 'completely absurd'.[13]

Eventually, in May 2021, the parliamentary Treasury Select Committee and the Public Accounts Committee began investigations into the former prime minister's lobbying on behalf of Greensill Capital, and found that he had breached no laws. He was cleared of all formal wrongdoing by the parliamentary committees, and therein lies the problem – there are no laws restricting Cameron or anyone in a similar position from doing the exact same thing again.

So, if something looks, smells and feels so utterly wrong, why is it so easy and so common in the British political scene? As David Cameron so eloquently put it in the 2010s – and so poignantly demonstrated in the 2020s – the quiet word in the ear, the ex-ministers for hire and the lunches and text messages to senior government officials are all part of the normal cycle of Westminster politics, and it's all there to help big business and billionaire bosses get their way.

The ease with which big business and the 1 per cent dominate British politics comes largely from the fact that transparency laws, as they relate to lobbying and influence in British politics, are woefully behind those of our Western neighbours. Unlike most of our allies, the US and Canada being some prominent examples, there are very few regulatory laws on lobbying in the UK. While tentative moves have been made since the turn of the 21st century to improve this, we still have some of the least transparent regulations in the world on the professional lobbying industry. In 2014 the government introduced legislation – years after promising to do so – which it claimed was going to increase transparency by creating a statutory register of lobbyists. This was, according to ministers, going to be a way for all members of the public to know who was talking to and influencing their public officials.

In reality, it is anything but that. The law only requires 'consultant lobbyists' to register, and only if they directly contact ministers and senior government officials. This means that of the 4,000 estimated lobbyists working in the UK, the register only accounts for around '90 organisations representing 300 or so clients'.[14] So, for most ordinary voters around the country, contrary to government spin, we still have no idea of who is meeting our representatives, what they are saying, who they are lobbying for and what impact this is having on legislation being written and passed in Parliament. The House of Commons Political and Constitutional Reform Committee itself made this clear as it stated that the lobbying register 'bill's definition of "consultancy lobbying" is flawed. Not only does it exclude in-house lobbyists, which was the Government's intention, but as currently drafted it would also exclude the vast majority of third party lobbyists, and particularly the larger organisations.'[15]

Even the coronavirus pandemic, a deadly and global problem that shut down most of the world and brought with it millions of deaths, was not immune to the cancerous influence of 'big money'. In the midst of one of the biggest and most urgent crises our country has faced since the Second World War, we saw the true face of financial corruption in our politics running wild, with no law or regulation holding it back. As the country wrestled with a new and deadly pandemic, infections rose and the healthcare system came under intense pressure, the Conservative government began handing out contracts to private companies on everything from personal protective equipment (PPE) to our national Test and Trace programme.

As months and weeks passed, not only was the delivery on these contracts by private providers shambolic, as doctors and nurses and care workers died without appropriate PPE, and Test and Trace had nearly no impact on community transmissions, but the process in which these contracts had been awarded was also exposed. Transparency International UK, an organisation fighting corruption worldwide, found that one in five government contracts awarded between February and November 2020 contained 'red flag indicators' of possible corruption.[16] Their report cited a 'seriously flawed' arrangement in government, where companies after big money contracts were placed in 'VIP lanes' often based on their political connections to the Tory party and senior ministers. The campaign group identified 73 'questionable contracts' worth in excess of £3.7 billion that warranted further investigation, of which £2.9 billion was for PPE[17] and 27 (PPE and testing) contracts that were awarded to firms with direct connections to the Conservative Party.[18]

Transparency International also found that £225 million's worth of contracts went to companies that had only been incorporated within the 60 days of tender, and many were awarded without a competitive tender process. In one particularly ludicrous example, a pub landlord won a multimillion-pound coronavirus contract after lobbying the then Health Secretary Matt Hancock at a local bar, and went on to buy a new luxury house.[19] Transparency International wrote quite tellingly that 'adopting such an approach adds credence to the view that cronyism determined the award of contracts, rather than suitability for the job. … This approach has undoubtedly damaged trust in the integrity of the pandemic response.'[20]

So, while we often reassure ourselves on these UK shores that 'big money' control of politics is an issue only for our friends across the Atlantic, it would seem the super-rich have it easier here, with far less rules and an open door to governments and prime ministers. UK politics, unlike that of its allies, is a relative lawless wild wild west for big money. Here, you can do almost anything you like; the public might not like it, they may even occasionally punish politicians for it at the ballot box, but there isn't a law or regulation in sight that will stand in your way.

★ ★ ★

It's not just that British politics is easier to buy (due to its lack of laws and regulations); it's cheaper too.

While some sigh with relief at the fact that there is far less money swirling around British politics, many others see it as an opportunity. An example: the 2018 US midterm elections were estimated to have cost almost US$6 billion. While an increasing amount of this figure would have been raised through small donations – due in large part to the rise of candidates such as Bernie Sanders and Elizabeth Warren – the majority of this financial war chest is still raised through millionaire and billionaire donors. So, while the likes of the Koch brothers and Robert Mercer spend billions of dollars gaining influence on the US political scene, here, in the UK, anyone with £50,000 burning a hole in their back pocket can join the Conservative Leader's Group and have dinner with the prime minister. In fact, a donation of £160,000 was enough to get a former Russian minister's wife an exclusive tennis match with Boris Johnson himself.[21]

Electoral Commission figures show that controversial luxury property developer Nick Candy and the London-based football team West Ham United owner David Sullivan were also donors, with the latter giving £75,000. All of which buys the time, ear and favour of the ruling party. So, in a world where it costs billions to buy influence in one system, and a few hundred thousand to buy sway in another, which do you choose? If we are honest, billionaires rarely have to choose – they just buy both, don't they?

Methods to safeguard and protect our democracy from this kind of influence have been around for decades and are not particularly radical. The introduction of donation caps, say, £10,000 per year, per person, per party, would force political parties and actors to rely on a far wider, more inclusive, donor base. This was highlighted by Sir Christopher Kelly, a former senior civil servant, who published a paper in November 2011 titled *Ending the big donor culture*.[22] Sir Christopher's paper highlighted that 'even £10,000 is high by international standards'; however, anything below that may be an 'over-reaction'. He also, importantly, highlighted that caps should apply to organisations and businesses too, as often the biggest money flows from multinational conglomerates. However, as he also alluded to, trade unions should be viewed differently as they are more a collection of individuals than a singular organisation. There is just no way we could reasonably associate Unite the Union and HSBC as one and the same.

But rather than take steps to safeguard and protect our democracy, in recent years we have moved in entirely the opposite direction. Boris Johnson's government has made moves to further deregulate and strip the Electoral Commission (the main election watchdog in the UK) of its power to prosecute law-breaking. In a move that conveniently followed an investigation into the controversial refurbishment of Boris's Downing Street flat, the government announced a new bill to remove the watchdog's ability to prosecute criminal offences under electoral law, branding it a 'waste of public money'.

This is the reality of 'big money' in politics. It not only maintains a vice-like grip on our systems, but also continues in its attempts to make life even easier for itself. For those of us seeking a healthy democratic process, where the volume of our voice isn't proportionate to the number of 0s in our bank account, we must recognise that this problem exists on our shores, and we need the will, ideas and basic courage to tackle it.

★ ★ ★

There is a common saying on the left of British politics: they (the Conservatives) have the money and we (Labour) have the people. It is a good saying and one I am certainly a subscriber to. The way we have always countered the open tap of big money flowing into right-wing political campaigns is to inspire and mobilise the masses to get our message out. But even with all the people in the world, with all their enthusiasm, energy and drive, when you are up against a Goliath-scale financial opponent, it is hard not to feel as though you are running in an impossible race.

By the summer of 2019 Boris Johnson's coronation as prime minister was complete, and our race had gone from a high-profile campaign to a complete media circus. The task facing our team was a very different prospect now – we had gone from looking to cause a huge national upset to being the first campaign in British democracy history to unseat a sitting prime minister. History was calling, except the cost of answering seemed increasingly beyond us.

Election spending laws in the UK are utterly confounding to most first-time candidates. Expenditure in the 'short campaign', a term used to describe the formal six- to seven-week campaigning period before polling day, is tightly regulated by the Electoral Commission. Spending caps are set in accordance with the number of electors in a constituency and encompass almost all campaign activities – from advertising materials to public meetings.

However, outside the 'short campaign' period, candidates and political parties are free to (and often do) spend whatever they like. As general elections are rarely called within six weeks of the given polling day, candidates often front-load their expenditure to land before the 'short campaign'. This, as well as a general political understanding across the parties of mutually assured destruction, means that the last time a general election candidate was convicted of breaking election spending limits in the UK was the 1920s.

Yet, despite this, our Monday campaign strategy meetings had slowly begun to change in both their focus and content. We spent more time discussing how to fund our activities, as opposed to what our activities should be specifically. While we had some success in fundraising, given our opponent's profile, the cost of running a campaign this large was beyond our relatively small constituency party. As a general rule, the Labour Party itself provides very little funds to support local parliamentary campaigns. Almost all of the money we had available for our campaign came from the local CLP (membership fees and donations), contributions from trade unions (namely my union, Unite) and donations from individuals around the country. Despite thousands of pounds raised locally, numbers that were unprecedented for a CLP of no more than 600 members, we still found ourselves constantly frustrated and held back.

Our financial limitations meant we often had to approach political problems creatively. We printed our leaflets and materials in smaller chunks so that we could get them cheaper. We made sure that our messaging was universal and not time-limited – to safeguard against reprinting and additional costs. I even remember specifically drying individual leaflets on the radiator, as they had been soaked the previous night in the rain, so that we could reuse them again at our following campaign sessions. We did not have a penny that could go to waste. Many of our most innovative and exciting ideas, from a mock Boris/Trump billboard to direct mail from me to all our constituents, found themselves axed at inception due to a lack of finances. Our digital campaign, which was a particular priority of mine, relied entirely on organic reach (not paid online advertisements). Where we had an approximate £200 a month digital budget, we estimated our Conservative opponents easily spending in the thousands (if not tens of thousands) in targeted advertisements online.

It was undeniable for anyone within our campaign: this was not an equal race. One of us was in a Ford Focus while the other was racing in a Ferrari.

★ ★ ★

Although political commentators and analysts are often focused on the influence of big money in politics, the effect of 'small money' is just as determinate in our political space. When we talk about 'small money', it is broadly a conversation about the financial capabilities of individuals involved in political spaces, and how personal wealth and class impact the kinds of actors that make up British politics.

For all of my adult life, through university and beyond, I had lived pay cheque to pay cheque. Having amassed a sizeable overdraft through my student years (due partly to having to send money back home every month), most months would see payday lift me out of thousands of pounds worth of debt only to slowly slip back by the beginning of the following month.

This is a story that would be unremarkable to most working-age Britons, one where the possibility of amassing any sizeable savings or having any serious disposable income always seems beyond reality. Yet, despite this material reality, I felt incredibly privileged. For most of the first half of our 14-month campaign, from being selected in September 2018 through to June 2019, I was working full time at the NUS. Having been re-elected to the post of Vice-President in March 2018, I was in an extremely privileged position of having a flexible full-time job that was able to accommodate a rigorous national campaign. Most of my duties could be designed around campaign responsibilities and allow me to fulfil both roles fully and with relative freedom. My colleagues at the NUS were supportive of my political activities, and often the two responsibilities would complement each other quite well.

But everything began to change as we passed through the summer of 2019. As Boris Johnson's premiership became official, and my own public profile began to rise, so, too, came growing financial insecurities and anxieties. My term as Vice-President of the NUS was due to end by July 2019, so I began to look for a new job through that spring and early into the summer. As CVs began to be sent out, applications filled in and interviews completed, I started noticing a consistent and alarming trend in my rejection feedback – no one wanted to touch a candidate taking on the country's prime minister.

Despite my extensive experience, having been a managing director of two multimillion-pound charities by the age of 24, most organisations and charities either did not want an overtly party political employee, or would not risk their work with government by having the prime minister's very public opponent on their payroll. While all of this was understandable logically, it left me nowhere to go. With very little savings and no access to the kind of familial wealth afforded the likes of Boris Johnson, I was staring down the barrel of financial abyss.

It looked like I had a last-minute reprieve when, in late June, I made it to the final interview stages at two different organisations. The first one, a campaigning NGO in the health sector, later withdrew their interest, citing my 'high public profile' involvement in 'Labour politics'; however, the second one – Stroke Association UK – offered me a public affairs position to begin in July. With a family history on the issue (my father had suffered a stroke in late 2005), I accepted and began organising my affairs. I worked on a schedule that would allow me to work full time and not miss any campaigning activities, began to discuss with the party how I would ensure there was no conflict of interest with my new position, and went out to buy new shirts and ties for my new role. Like a kid going to start high school, I was excited by the prospect of being able to work and campaign again.

On the morning of 28 June, having completed referencing and signing an employment contract, and getting ready to begin work in a matter of days, I received a call from the HR department. Following the public announcement of my employment, an anonymous source had been in touch with the organisation's bosses to highlight my public position and my previous public comments. They had pointed out the coverage of these comments by right-wing papers, and scared the organisation as to what impact my presence would have on their work. As I heard this explained on the phone, I sat up on the corner of my bed. Alone in my flat, on a Thursday morning, I listened tentatively as the HR rep explained that it would be too difficult for the organisation to go through with the appointment and that they would have to withdraw their offer and terminate my already signed contract. I felt all the energy and enthusiasm drain from my body. I was now unemployed and seemingly unemployable, with little savings and a world of responsibilities, and without reason to hope for the future.

I sat there for a while, feeling hopeless and with a combination of both anger and fear. Why was I being punished for a high profile that came with being a candidate and wanting to stand up for my community? How could it be this difficult? How could I go on?

I looked down at my phone and opened my mobile banking app. After some quick maths and financial calculations, I figured out exactly how bad the situation was. If things went on exactly as they had been going for the months preceding, I had just six weeks. Six weeks before I would lose my flat, be without a penny to my name and unable to continue this fight. For only the second time in the whole campaign, I thought about dropping out of the race.

'It's not worth it', I thought, 'the price is just too damn high'.

★ ★ ★

Elections are expensive operations. Not just for national and local parties, but more than anything, for individual candidates. The cost of travel, election materials, clothes, food and so much more means that candidates like me, with no access to serious disposable income and familial wealth, often fall into serious hardship. Among the pool of parliamentary candidates heading into the 2019 election, it was commonplace to hear stories of serious financial hardship. At one gathering I heard of a candidate remortgaging their family home to pay their way through a campaign. At another conference, we got wind of another candidate facing bankruptcy as a result of the rising costs of the campaign and the loss of their job due to their new position within the party.

At a local level, money as a variable is probably the single most exclusionary factor in candidates running. Without the ability to divorce your employment from your political career, the financial freedom to take huge amounts of time off to campaign, and the economic freedom to spend large amounts of money on campaign materials, it is almost impossible to mount a serious political campaign in any constituency.

If you are a parent – particularly a single parent or with young kids – you are likely to find it impossible to spend three or four hours of the afternoon out on the campaign trail six days of the week. If you are a carer and have caring responsibilities for someone in your life, you are certainly not going to be able to dedicate most of your time outside work to knocking on doors and attending campaign events. And if you, like me, just can't afford not to work, you are unlikely to be able to take such a high-profile partisan public role, where the likelihood of ending up on the front page of *The Sun* or *Daily Mail* is generally quite high.

It can therefore be of no surprise to any of us that a large part of our elected representatives and parliamentary candidates in this country are often richer, older individuals, with both the money and the time to participate in the electoral process. This is clearly reflected in make-up of the House of Commons across all parties. Analysis by Oliver Heath for the London School of Economics and Political Science and Cambridge University Press found that over the past 50 years, the number of working-class representatives has steadily declined in British politics. In 1964, around 20 per cent of parliamentarians had come from a working-class occupational background, but by the 2010s that number had fallen to just 5 per cent.[23,24] This decline is also almost entirely due to the changes that have occurred within the Labour Party: 'In 1964, Labour was not just a party for the working class, but was also a party that was substantially comprised of the working class, with over 37 per cent of the MPs coming from manual occupational backgrounds. By 2010 this fell to just under 10 per cent.'[25]

The percentage of MPs who are manual workers, such as miners or electricians, has decreased steadily over the past 35 years – from 16 per cent to just 4 per cent. The proportion of teachers and educators has also fallen, from 7.9 per cent in 1979 to just 2.6 per cent in 2015; as has the number of farmers – 3.7 per cent to 1.1 per cent over the same period.[26] While only 2 per cent of the adult UK population are landlords owning property, 39 per cent of Tory MPs, 26 per cent of SNP (Scottish National Party) MPs and 22 per cent of Labour MPs were landlords as of 2016. Almost 19 per cent of people in the UK have a disability, whereas less than 0.5 per cent of MPs have self identified as having a disability.[27] All the while, the number of MPs who came from 'white-collar' professions, such as executives and solicitors, has increased by 9.8 per cent and 3.4 per cent respectively.

It's safe to say that this Parliament looks nothing like us, because it is not made up of us. The influence of both 'small money' and 'big money' has created a revolving door of middle- and upper-class, rich, older, often white MPs who have the financial capabilities to run and win parliamentary selections and elections. And worst of all, it's as much a problem in the Labour Party as anywhere else.

Most people don't know that as a political candidate you don't get paid to stand. In fact, financial support from either the state or the Labour Party is virtually nonexistent. Throughout the entirety of the campaign, we received next to no money from the national Labour Party that made any real substantial difference to our work. Most of the cost fell on our local party and very often on our local team. It starts off small. A few leaflets here and there. A hall booking for an event. The cost of travel to and from campaign events. But over the course of 18 months, it becomes a staggeringly unaffordable endeavour, and it is one of the most inaccessible parts of our political process.

While the UK is one of the few countries that does have public financing of political parties – mostly through 'short money' – this rarely trickles down to opposition parties' individual candidates as a way of opening up the accessibility of running for public office. The primary public financing of political parties in the UK is through 'short money'. 'Short money', named after former Labour MP Edward Short, was established in 1975 to support opposition parties in carrying out their business. Its main function is to ensure a healthy opposition and thus a healthy democracy. 'Short money' is available to any opposition party that wins more than two seats in the House of Commons:

> At the start of the 2019/20 fiscal year, general funding to opposition parties under the Short Money scheme was allocated as follows: £18,044.80 per seat won by the party at the last election and £36.04 multiplied by 1/200th of the number of votes the party received in the same election. A lump sum for travel expenses was divided between the opposition parties in the same proportion as the amount given under the general funding scheme.[28]

Public financing of politics, although with its drawbacks, is an obvious place to start in rooting out what Anne Applebaum described as a political environment where 'untransparent money, from unknown sources, is widely accepted with a complacent shrug'.[29] A combination of robust transparency laws on private donors, strict caps on private donations and a healthy and fair public financing of political parties and campaigning is the sort of balance we should be striving for in our political sphere. However, as my story and the story of those I met along the way makes clear, conversations around money and politics cannot start with those already in Westminster and in public office. It starts long before then. It starts with those who dropped out, who never even stood, who were driven out of public service because of their financial circumstances.

There is no doubt that all across the country we are losing good and decent people, who would make fantastic public servants, because they are working class, because they are single parents, because they cannot participate in our inaccessible political processes, and because they don't have access to the same financial security the likes of Boris Johnson, David Cameron and Jacob Rees-Mogg have been afforded their whole life. And this has a very real impact on the realities of our politics. It is impossible to expect politics to represent us all, when its actors come exclusively from one set of people. It is equally impossible to expect our politics to change or for there to be any significant shift away from the status quo, if decisions are made by those who have, for all their lives, benefited from the status quo.

If my campaign, journey and story has taught me one thing, it's that our politics has to change. Not just in policy, but in process. Not just in rhetoric, but in structure. This can only be done if we elect leaders who come from our communities, who understand us, and who know what it's like to live like us.

7

'This is big. Bigger than me'

It was a cold, wet, Tuesday evening.

As I leaned against the damp exterior of South Ruislip Station, I could feel a rush of anxiety and regret. This was so stupid, I thought to myself. Why would we host a campaign rally outside a major constituency train station, in the middle of the week, in these cold and wet conditions? Obviously, no one was coming.

South Ruislip Station is one of the busiest train stations in all of Uxbridge and South Ruislip. As the major connector between our outer West London district and the heart of the city, it is one of the main stations used by workers this side of London. It had, for this reason, also been one of our most frequent campaigning spots. We had held canvassing sessions, leaflet drops and even attempted to buy advertisement space on a major billboard adjacent to the main station entranceway.

So when the time came to host another major campaign rally, it was a natural choice.

Uxbridge and South Ruislip, as the name suggests, is often split into two main geographical locations. Separated by a major highway that runs through the two distinct areas, it is essentially two different constituencies combined into one. In the south we have Uxbridge, the more densely populated, working-class area – where I lived. In the north was South Ruislip, a more suburban and middle-class area, that is greener in appearance and bluer in politics.

Traditionally, the Labour Party had done next to no general election campaigning in the north of the constituency. The three wards in the north (South Ruislip, Cavendish and Manor) were Conservative strongholds, and so previous candidates and campaigns had focused their efforts and resources on where they believed they were more likely to find success. This was a reasonable strategy, as all our data and polling suggested most of Labour's vote had been concentrated in the south.

However, we weren't willing to give up on the north of the constituency. James Clouting, our campaign organiser, often reminded us that in the last local council elections, over 700 people in his ward in the north had voted Labour. This was without a single knock on the door or interaction with one of our campaigners: 'If 700 people are willing to come out and vote for Labour without any campaigning, we can surely get more if we put some effort in.' When we looked at the data in our campaign database, and at our conversations with voters at canvassing sessions, it had become apparent that in some of these areas, the Labour Party had not spoken to them in nearly a decade. I was the first Labour candidate they had seen since the days of Gordon Brown.

So, when Owen Jones approached us to host one of his national Labour campaign rallies, it made sense for us to use the opportunity to make up for many lost years in the north. It was our second 'Unseat Boris Johnson' event, following from our first outside Hillingdon Civic Centre a few months prior, and was likely to attract a lot of press attention. At this point, anything we did was covered in some way by the press.

In the past few months we had begun venturing to the north of the constituency – much to the chagrin of local Tory activists – and all our campaign activities had been surprisingly positive. As a historically strong base for Boris Johnson and the Conservatives, we were definitely feeling a significant shift away from the prime minister – dissent towards his handling of the Brexit negotiations, anger at the decisions to prorogue Parliament and, most importantly, frustration at the little time he had spent in his own constituency. In a lot of people's minds, it came down to who they were most likely to have a conversation with. One candidate was on their doorstep, another on their TV screens.

Owen's extremely busy diary meant that the only available date that worked for us all was on a Tuesday. As James, Andy and Jane began to put together the details for the rally, there was hesitation from all of us about what kind of turnout we would have. Our campaign had picked up a life of its own, and attendance at our rallies and our volunteer numbers were unprecedented – some of the highest, if not *the* highest in the country. But most of that came on weekends, bank holidays and the occasional school holidays.

Andy was the first to raise reservations at one of our weekly Monday campaign meetings: 'Asking people to travel to South Ruislip in the middle of the week for an evening rally with work the next day might be too much, even for us.' Campaign agent Norrette agreed and also had reservations around the weather: 'Looks like it's going to be a wet one too.'

Norrette's concern was around focus. Organising an event of this scale would require our attention and resources, and it would mean directing efforts away from our day-to-day campaigning that had brought so much success. We had convinced thousands of voters to support us not by big rallies, but by the daily grind of the campaign – knocking on doors, delivering leaflets, organising town hall and community outreach events. This was potentially a big distraction.

But we also knew it to be a big opportunity. The first 'Unseat' rally we had held was a major boost for the campaign and spread the word in the local area. We needed something equally big in the north. We didn't want it to appear that we favoured the south just because most of our votes were concentrated there.

There was another element that was on my mind that I didn't verbalise with the team. We needed to reassure those 'maybe' voters that this was the real deal. A big, visible show of strength in South Ruislip could provide comfort to those previous Conservative voters who were considering switching, but who may have thought an opponent to Boris could not win.

Ultimately, we pressed on with the event.

As I stood at South Ruislip Station, with the rain trickling down my forehead, looking out at the empty patch of grass we were due to host our rally on in just over an hour, I felt a crippling anxiety, the kind I had not felt at any point in the election so far. I could see the conditions around me. It was wet, it was cold, it was dark; there was just no way we would get any significant numbers at this rally.

I also knew that the press would be coming, two major left-wing commentators in the form of Owen Jones and Ash Sarkar would be coming, and many of our most loyal local volunteers would also be there, and if we had an embarrassingly low turnout, as seemed inevitable, this could be the end of all the momentum we had worked so hard to build. Our opponent meant we didn't have the luxury of making mistakes. One look at an empty rally, and everyone would quickly reach a quite logical conclusion: 'There's no way this guy is going to beat a prime minister.'

I felt my heart race and my breathing get heavy. I was angry and embarrassed. Frustrated and annoyed. All at myself, all at once.

Had I let all of this get to my head? All this attention and notoriety had made me lose focus. Had I just ruined the hard work of so many dedicated local volunteers? Would this affect the incredible campaign team we had built over the last year? It was too late now – no turning back.

I rushed into a local coffee shop to find a public restroom. The panic had set in now and I felt as though I was going to vomit. I had to pull myself together. With James, Andy and Jane all busy organising the rally that afternoon, I had set up some media interviews to take place just before the rally. The evening event had meant no campaigning that afternoon, and an opportunity for us to catch up on some press engagements. The one thing I did not need now was to bomb an interview ahead of this rally.

A quick splash of water to the face, a few deep breaths, and off we went. The first engagement was a TV interview with a German news outlet. Then there was a phone interview with the *Evening Standard*. And last, we were back in the coffee shop for a profile interview I had agreed to do with Sirin Kale for *VICE*.

One lesson I had to learn quickly now that our campaign had so much attention and was in the spotlight was the need for me to be 'on' all the time. I always had to be in candidate mode, smiling, confident, leading our team to success. The level of scrutiny and micro-inspection, especially for a young Muslim candidate taking on an establishment figure, meant there was no room for 'off' days. I was never allowed moments of worry, of fear, of uncertainty. Any of these feelings had to be dealt with in an instant, on my own, and suppressed, always ready for the next engagement.

I saw this as ultimately one of my responsibilities. The campaign was not mine; it belonged to everyone who had built it with me. From our core team of James, Andy, Jane and Norrette, to some of our most loyal campaigners, Dee Stuart, Tim Slattery, Ray Meen, and so many more. This all belonged to them as much as it did me. So the slightest misstep from me, or moments of vulnerability, wouldn't just be followed by attacks on 'Ali Milani the individual', but a campaign that had been built by so many. I was not prepared to let that happen.

The interviews all went well. By this late stage in the campaign I had found doing press engagements quite easy. I told our story, stressed the historic nature of the campaign and pointed to a future that could be unlocked if we could defeat Boris Johnson in Uxbridge and South Ruislip.

As we left the coffee shop and began to walk back towards South Ruislip Station, we heard a commotion, like the sound of the quiet, collective chatter you would find in a theatre before the show was underway. The closer we got, the louder it got. Then, as we reached the entrance to the station, we saw people, everywhere.

At first, when I saw the enormous crowd gathered on the same spot we had planned our rally, I was confused. There were what looked like 400–500 people crammed onto a patch of grass, circling round a single tree protecting them from the rain. The people were tailed by huge cameras and bright spotlights. At first I thought that the station had been evacuated, but then I saw people coming in and out of it, more people, like a trail of worker ants making their way to the same spot as the rest of the crowd.

With a quick glance I found Andy frantically gathering leaflets and campaign sheets across the road. 'What's all this?' I approached and asked him, as it slowly began to sink in. I just wanted someone to confirm what I was seeing. 'What are all these people doing here?' Andy broke his rapid organising energy for just a moment, placed a hand on my shoulder, and with a warm smile told me: 'They're here for you mate.'

Looking out at the crowd, I was emotional. This was big, way bigger than me.

I could see that we had accomplished something special. We had built a campaign, a story that had inspired so many. It wasn't about one candidate but what is and isn't possible in our country. People had placed their own dreams and hopes in this race, in this Labour Party.

★ ★ ★

South Ruislip was a shot in the arm for the campaign. It not only transformed the way others saw us, but also the way we saw ourselves. It was the moment that I, privately, started to actually believe. We might just be able to pull this off.

From that rally on, every public campaigning session we ran became a rally. The numbers of volunteers flocking from around the country was truly unprecedented for a local marginal seat. We bumped the number of sessions to three a day – morning, afternoon and evening. Full speed ahead.

Our campaign operation had also become a seamless machine. Andy organised all the administrative elements of where we would be and what voter-ID data we used. I attended every session and led them with a typical stump speech and knocked on doors right alongside the volunteers. James followed my speeches with training for every volunteer who needed it, coordinating them into teams. And Jane input the thousands of responses and vote promises we got on the doorstep into our digital campaign system. It was a well-oiled machine.

I had begun to get into the habit of asking people to shout out how far they had come from at the beginning of my stump speech. It began with visitors from neighbouring boroughs – Harrow, Ealing, Southall and so on. As time went on, it got further and further – Brighton, Nottingham, Edinburgh, Bristol. And then it began to get outrageous – campaigners flying in from Amsterdam, Brussels and even New York, to knock on doors for us.

I remember a group of young people who had flown in from Scandinavia after seeing the coverage of our race in their local press. They had planned a trip to London because they believed that the fight for a better world did not end at their borders or their isles. It was a global fight, and one they wanted to have a say in. So they came to Uxbridge and helped us knock on doors and speak to voters for a weekend.

More than most others, my generation understands that politics in the modern world cannot be seen just through the prism of individual nations. The scale of the challenges facing us requires an international, collective effort. The crisis of climate change, the resurgence of fascism and the war-imposed refugee crisis, these all need cooperation and collaboration across countries and continents. These issues cannot be solved alone.

Nothing better exemplifies the need for politics to change in this regard than the coronavirus pandemic. The deadly, global pandemic, that first hit hard in early 2020, brought our global economy and the way of life we had come to know to its knees.

This disease, in just a few months, showed us with extraordinary clarity that the problems of the next decade would not just be contained within our singular nations. As COVID-19 spread throughout every country, it became apparent that what was required was an international effort, to both contain its spread and to develop vaccines. Much of the failures, and so many of the deaths, came about due to a catastrophic failure by leaders to take this approach.

As richer countries hoarded PPE, most of the rest of the world saw a desperate shortage. As vaccinations became available, nations refused to release patents, bought up global supplies and left developing countries with next to no real vaccine roll-out programmes. The *British Medical Journal* reported that on the global vaccinations roll-out, we had fallen desperately short, 'with the G7 nations committing to only one billion vaccines in the coming year, well short of the 11 billion needed'.[1]

These failures, and so many more, have led to the uncontrolled spread of the virus in Brazil, Britain, India and beyond, and caused more virulent variants and ultimately millions of deaths.

But among the examples are also stories of success, inspiring leaders ready and willing to show tremendous solidarity across borders to address these issues. Take the #BlackLivesMatter (BLM) movement. 'Seven years ago, we were called together', recalls Professor Melina Abdullah from Los Angeles. 'There were about 30 of us standing in the courtyard of this black artist community in Los Angeles, summoned by Patrisse Cullors, one of our co-founders and one of my dearest friends. It was students … artists, organisers and mommas.'[2]

Seven years later, and after the brutal murder of George Floyd by a police officer in Minneapolis, their movement had spread far beyond the courtyards of Los Angeles.

The summer of 2020 saw protests and community actions beyond even the US and into London, Brussels, Seoul, Sydney, Monrovia, Rio de Janeiro and beyond. The BLM call had become a global one. It was now not just the rallying cry against police brutality in the US, but also a voice against racial injustice across the world. It saw athletes taking the knee, communities taking to the streets and mainstream media scrambling to understand where this had come from. BLM provided a platform for an international generation to become collectively conscious of our world's history, the systematic oppressions, the institutional racism and the need for collective, international action.

That same energy has panned across the world in recent years with the actions of young people over the existential threat of climate change. Over 2 million walked out of schools and workplaces, and 6 million took to the streets in 2019, 'uniting across timezones, cultures and generations to demand urgent action on the escalating ecological emergency'.[3] They brought together the voices of young and old, across nations, to demand not just a future for themselves, but also for the planet as a whole.

Even those who study social protests have gone on the record to say that the manner in which the youth organise globally today is unprecedented:

> At a time of fraying trust in authority figures, children – who by definition have no authority over anything – are increasingly driving the debate. Using the internet, young people are organizing across continents like no generation before them. And though their outsize demands for an end to fossil fuels mirror those of older environmentalists, their movement has captured the public imagination far more effectively.[4]

This is a new world, with new challenges, and the struggles of today and tomorrow can only be tackled together. If the far-right, populist, nationalists are going to have a cooperative global network, then so will we. The axis of Donald Trump, Vladimir Putin, Narendra Modi and Boris Johnson needs an equal international progressive response.

As a candidate, this was not a particularly alien concept to me. I had been inspired along the way by many stories I had seen from across the world. Even before our primary race, the gubernatorial race in Michigan involving candidate Abdul el-Sayed had inspired me. In Abdul's story, I saw myself. Seeing him taking on an establishment figure of the Democratic Party reassured me that it was possible. Alexandria Ocasio-Cortez's rise to prominence was also often discussed in our campaign. Many believed that a win in Uxbridge and South Ruislip would have propelled our campaign to the heights hers had reached. And I watched her deal with the attention, scrutiny and responsibility with remarkable authenticity, maintaining her community roots and the political courage to advocate for her community. These leaders were just as influential on my thinking and confidence as any in the UK.

We had also seen my opponent's global solidarity network in full strength. There were consistent reports throughout the latter parts of the campaign of Boris Johnson receiving advice and support from a range of right-wing political actors, including Steve Bannon. Bannon was the mastermind behind the Donald Trump campaign and founding member of the far-right news, opinion and political commentary website Breitbart.

The world today is a very small place. We can therefore assume that all of this is the natural progression of politics in an increasingly globalised world. Our economies, trade, security and data are more interconnected than at any time in human history. The rapid emergence of new technologies has also brought countries, nations and people closer together than ever before.

Perspectives often vary as they relate to globalisation in modern politics, but broadly globalisation is defined as 'the intensification of social relations, exchange of cultures and compression of distance. Globalization can be defined by one's own point of view. An economist can define it through global flow of capital and extension of market. A musician can define it as hybridization of culture and a politician can define it as increase of interdependence of states.'[5]

Some will argue that while the means in which we communicate and relate to one another have changed, the nature of these relations hasn't much changed. They claim that while the tools we use have changed, the essence of our politics hasn't. States continue to have supreme authority of their own borders and domestic affairs and today's world is not a 'globalised' one but a more 'internationalised' one.[6]

But this doesn't see modern politics in its full picture. Politics today isn't just the actions and behaviours of a collection of states as cold, lifeless institutions, but rather the behaviours, beliefs and actions of people all across the world.

You could see this new world in the Arab Spring, for example. As people took to the streets across nations and borders to fight for a freer and fairer society, they inspired one another. They used technology and networks to discuss strategies and plans. They organised together and won together. We saw this new world as women from across nations united behind the #MeToo movement to highlight and fight against misogyny, sexism and patriarchy in politics and society as a whole.

Many of these movements that started in one locale and quickly spread beyond borders and into the realm of the global have seen government and corporate policies crumble quite quickly. These changes haven't come through the wisdom of domestic actors supremely in control, but rather, global movements that had pushed the narrative far enough to where decision-makers needed to act (for their own survival).

Ultimately, I saw this new world in the faces of the crowds that attended our rallies and campaign sessions. They saw our campaign, and Ali Milani as a candidate, not just as a means of improving the lives of those in Uxbridge and South Ruislip, but also of playing a part (even if a small one) in changing the narrative around the world. Just as Alexandria Ocasio-Cortez had in New York. Just as Ilhan Omar had in Minneapolis.

And that gave me hope, that we were ready to meet the challenges ahead. Because there is a new generation of activists, unburdened by the past, ready to build a cooperative, collaborative and international movement.

* * *

The buoyant energy behind the campaign had not just attracted the attention of the media and volunteers, but now, it had also attracted the attention of MPs.

Initially the presence of MPs was quite exciting. Having support from the likes of John McDonnell, Rebecca Long-Bailey and Richard Burgon was not only good for the morale of our immediate local volunteers, but also for attracting new campaigners to our patch in West London. It also gave me a personal boost of confidence. Standing alongside seasoned campaigners, who had come not because they had to but because they wanted to, got me through the early grind of the campaign – the days where often no one showed up.

But, of course, by this point in the autumn, we were in a much different place.

The race in Uxbridge and South Ruislip was alive – thousands of volunteers each month, travelling across the country and even the world, to make our dream a reality, to be part of history. This was often what I would end my stump speech with. Before the volunteers went out, I would remind them of their role in this endeavour:

> This race is going to be close. I can tell you that now with absolute certainty. Whatever happens on election night, we know it is going to be one of the closest fights a sitting prime minister has ever had in their own seat. And I want you to remember that today. As you knock on the doors, as you speak to families, and as you go street by street, I want you to remember, that one conversation you had, that one person you convinced, that could just be the difference.
>
> I might be stood on that stage on election night, with the whole world watching, and the announcement is made by the returning officer that Uxbridge and South Ruislip is a Labour gain. By

one vote, or two, or three. And that would be the door you knocked on. It would be the voter you convinced. That victory will belong more to you than it does to me. So let's go out and make history together. Let's make Boris Johnson the first sitting prime minister in the history of British democracy to lose his own constituency seat. Let's show the world what politics can be.

These moments were special. Although the crowds had grown enormously over the past few months, there was an incredible intimacy in our rallies. Looking out at the faces of the crowds, I could almost feel their hopes and dreams. I saw a glimpse of what politics could be. A vehicle for change. A vessel for people to come together and make better the lives of their families, their communities and their country.

We began hosting more and more parliamentarians at our events, although now, it often felt less like a show of support, and more a photo opportunity for some of them. A few would come to the rallies, give their speeches, and quickly head home before our canvassing sessions – although not before taking the necessary selfie to let the world know later that they had been in Boris Johnson's constituency to boot him out of Parliament. Others insisted we disrupt our entire campaigning schedule to suit them. On one occasion, I had to personally call Labour Party HQ and ask a shadow minister *not* to attend, as he had insisted we cancel our entire day's events and reorganise an event to fit around his brief and his calendar. This would often then involve the MP calling party officials and using quite colourful language about me, which was, of course, always reported back to me by members of staff with a giggle.

Our campaign was also host to most of the figures who would go on to stand to be leader and deputy leader of the Labour Party following Jeremy Corbyn's resignation in 2020. Almost all of them, at some point, came through our journey in Uxbridge and South Ruislip. More than one implicitly suggested to me in private conversations their intentions to stand, and one even had the audacity to ask for my support if they were going to stand.

I shouldn't have been surprised, but I was. These were some of the same people who had spent the best part of Jeremy Corbyn's leadership campaign attempting to 'break the man' and sabotaging our own electoral chances. I was furious – to be thinking about your own career prospects in the midst of our election fight, to be, by implication, predicting a Labour loss, was as close to treasonous as I could think of. In my anger, I remember vividly telling a member of our campaign committee – just before I was due to deliver my stump speech – that I had been quietly asked for my support in a future election. I leaned in, just before walking to the front of the crowd, and whispered: 'I didn't know we had already lost this election. I guess we're the idiots out here actually trying to get Labour to win an election.'

Despite a contingent of the PLP insisting we focus more on massaging their own egos than campaigning, there were others who were incredibly giving, easy to work with and there with the intention of furthering our local campaign. Richard Burgon and Rebecca Long-Bailey were two standouts, making themselves available, participating in press engagements and working selflessly for the benefit of our volunteers and our campaigners. Louise Hague was another, showing up without fuss for an afternoon event, knocking on doors right alongside our campaigners and even recording a digital advert for us on policing and crime.

Emily Thornberry, our shadow foreign affairs secretary, was another of the easier politicians to work with. She had agreed to attend one of our big events in Uxbridge town and, on the day, happened to show up earlier than we had expected. Not being ready, I called her and let her know we were at Andy's house having dinner and would be heading out shortly. Where others would have kicked up a fuss, Emily simply offered to join us and head into the campaign session with us.

As we all sat around in Andy's kitchen, garlic bread and doughnuts in hand (not at the same time, we aren't animals!), I thought about how far we had come. I thought back to that first day, sat on the bollard in Hillingdon East, alone, embarrassed, scared of the journey ahead. Now, we had hundreds of volunteers waiting for us on this day, the shadow foreign affairs secretary in Andy's kitchen (which now doubled up as campaign

HQ), and a line of press wanting interviews and pictures. I was momentarily speechless. As we prepared to head out, I saw Andy in the corridor. 'Can you believe this?' I asked him with an almost emotional break in my voice.

'I know mate, long way, but I really believe we can win this now.'

We couldn't afford too much time to take it all in. Not just because of the pace of the campaigning, but because of what was to come.

Boris's premiership was supposed to unlock Brexit, but it did nothing of the sort. Parliament was just as deadlocked as during Theresa May's tenure. No one could figure out what Brexit should look like, or whether it should even happen. It became clear that there was only one way out of this: a new Parliament.

On Tuesday 29 October 2019, the House of Commons passed the 2019 Early Parliamentary General Election Act.[7] We had seen it coming for a few days before, as Boris Johnson had called for a new election in the face of defeats on the floor of the House of Commons. But the pendulum really swung when smaller parties such as the SNP also indicated their willingness to support an early election.

I sat alone in my car, on the second floor car park of Harrow on the Hill shopping centre, and watched the vote on my phone. As the MPs approached the speaker, nodded their heads and read the results, I felt an immediate injection of emotion – fear, excitement, panic and determination. As the Act passed and an early general election was confirmed, I put down my phone and looked out of the window at the sky. This journey, this story, this incredible rollercoaster that had begun on 28 September 2018, was going to come to an end 440 days later.

Thursday, 12 December 2019 was election day.

8

'The audacity to dream of change'

This was our race to the finish, the conclusion of our rollercoaster journey. It was all coming to an end, one way or another, on 12 December 2019. Everything was different now. When we looked back at our campaign, our team and even me as a candidate, it was all unrecognisable compared to that first day over a year ago.

Our campaign machine was moving at light-speed now, every moment of every day filled with an engagement of some sort. Most of our mornings were filled with team leaflet drops, delivering targeted messages to specific neighbourhoods across the constituency. By the early afternoon, I would head over and meet James to lead our teams of volunteers out on canvassing sessions, knocking on doors and picking up last-minute votes in target wards.

Over lunch, I completed our media engagements – a few conversations with journalists on the phone, some interviews filmed near our next campaign destination, and the occasional race into a studio and back in time for the evening. The evenings were the most exciting parts of our day. They would most often see us host rallies of varying sizes around the constituency. Hundreds, sometimes thousands, of supporters and volunteers joined us on our election journey every week, fighting alongside us for this new political world we were hoping to create.

The energy that Jeremy Corbyn had built around the Labour Party – particularly within young people and those previously unengaged in politics – was undeniable. For all the criticisms and attacks laid at his door, one thing he has never truly got credit for is the way he inspired a new generation of activists.

I saw the result of his work in my own rallies and campaign events, faces showing up who had never been on a Labour doorstep before, people who had never dreamed of voting, let alone of campaigning, out fighting alongside us. For them, Jeremy Corbyn's Labour Party was a window into a new political reality.

This new reality was not just Jeremy's to hold; it was all of ours now. When Jeremy first won the Labour Party leadership race in 2015, it was a message shot ferociously across Westminster politics, a roar that would be heard by people like me. If he could win, we could win. If he could stand, we could stand. Whether you agreed with his politics or not, Jeremy had unlocked in the minds of millions what might be possible in politics. He had accomplished a feat as rare as they come in the political realm: he had inspired.

And you could also now see it in the election candidates. Faiza Shaheen, a young Muslim woman in Chingford and Wood Green, standing against Iain Duncan Smith, one of the architects of the Tory austerity programme. Faiza's tremendous charisma and enthusiastic campaign inspired me from afar and kept us on our toes. We often traded volunteers on weekends, with Labour activists travelling the country, and indeed the world, to spend a Saturday in Chingford and a Sunday in Uxbridge. Hundreds of first-time volunteers told me, day in, day out, that their biggest dream on election night was to turn on the TV and see Faiza and Ali beat Boris and Iain. That, for them, would be its own political revolution.

There were so many more – candidates such as Zarah Sultana in Coventry, Charlotte Nichols in Warrington North, Bell Ribeiro-Addy in Streatham, Apsana Begum in Poplar and Limehouse, and beyond. Pictured together, this class of leaders could not be further from the traditional image of an MP. Young, diverse, dynamic, exciting, these candidates looked more like the faces you would see pass you by in Streatham, or Poplar, or Coventry, or even Uxbridge.

They were people who understood what it was like to live like us. Why? Because they had lived like us, because they were one of us. This was a glimpse into what politics could be. Not a conveyor belt of Boris Johnsons and David Camerons, straight out of the Eton common rooms and into public office, but a House of Commons made up of real people, with real experiences and real connections to communities, most of whom had been inspired to join the Labour Party by Jeremy.

I tried to remind Jeremy of this running into him in the LOTO (insider term for 'Leader of the Opposition') offices late in the autumn. After finishing up a chat with John McDonnell down the hall and getting one last pep talk before the general election, we ran into Jeremy on our way out. Jacket off, with a bright white shirt and sleeves rolled up, Jeremy looked like he had either just come from an intensely difficult meeting or was headed out for a fight. At this point in the campaign, both were equally possible.

As I approached him to say a brief hello on my way out of the building, his expression instantly changed. A warmth took over his face as he took me by the shoulders and asked me how the campaign was going. He told me he had really enjoyed our bulldozer event. This was in reference to a campaign stunt in which I had laid in front of a bulldozer in Uxbridge town centre, to mimic Boris Johnson's previous broken promise to lay in front of the bulldozers that would build a third runway at Heathrow. Unfortunately, the way we had taken the pictures and my hesitancy at getting my suit wet on the floor meant that the picture came out far more, how can I put this ... salacious than we had intended. It became a popular meme on social media and I did my best to ignore the embarrassing incident.

Many things could be said about Jeremy, and many criticisms made about his leadership style, but one area he was undeniably gifted in was his one-to-one interactions. His warm smile and intense focus on what you were saying made you feel as though you were the only person in the room. He really made you sense that he cared, a skill as valuable as kryptonite for a politician. It was, in my opinion, the most influential quality that had brought him to the leader's office.

Yet behind his warm smile and attempts to talk shop about my campaign, I could sense the weight of leadership and responsibility on him. I recognised it now more than I had before. It was a feeling I had become familiar with – on a much smaller scale, and with a lot less scrutiny, I could see the pain of constant microscopic attention on your every movement, the scars of attack piece after attack piece in the press. Very few political leaders in modern history have faced the scale of onslaught Jeremy received in his tenure as leader. A report in the *Independent* found that 75 per cent of press coverage 'misrepresents Jeremy Corbyn' in the first year of his leadership.[1] 75 per cent!

A similar report by the London School of Economics and Political Science found that the Labour leader had been 'systematically ridiculed, scorned and the object of personal attacks by most newspapers'.[2] They went on to find that the 'degree of viciousness and antagonism with which the majority of the British newspapers have treated Corbyn is deemed to be highly problematic from a democratic perspective'.[3]

> [A]n overall picture of most newspapers systematically vilifying the leader of the biggest opposition party, assassinating his character, ridiculing his personality and delegitimising his ideas and politics. As the quote of Miliband Sr at the outset of this report already pointed out, this is not an entirely new phenomenon in the UK and has happened before in relation to other leftwing leaders from Neil Kinnock to Ed Miliband (see Curran, et al., 2005; Gabor, 2014), but in the case of Corbyn the degree of antagonism and hatred from part of the media has arguably reached new heights.[4]

We had all become used to it by 2019, but the truth is that the intensity of the personal attacks spread across the newspaper pages was beyond a healthy democracy. This wasn't a question of accountability – there was plenty to hold Jeremy to account for. There was a lot that even I disagreed with. But much of the coverage wasn't about accountability. They were vicious, personal, vindictive attacks on the man himself, full of malice.

The two headlines that have always stuck with me as best highlighting the hysteria surrounding Jeremy in the press were both on LBC, one of the UK's largest radio stations, which ran the following:

Jeremy Corbyn champions universal benefits with free school meals policy. Is this the nasty face of Corbyn's Labour?[5]

Jeremy Corbyn says PM should come clean over family finances after Panama leak. Should Corbyn resign over this call?[6]

Even David Dimbleby, one of the UK's most respected journalists, and the face of election night coverage, admitted as much: 'I don't think anyone could say that Corbyn has had a fair deal at the hands of the press, in a way that the Labour Party did when it was more to the centre, but then we generally have a rightwing press.'[7]

Knowing we wouldn't have any real time together, I held Jeremy right above the elbow. I leaned in to remind him that no matter what happened in a few weeks' time, 'None of us would be here if you hadn't inspired us to.' The confidence, the audacity, the belief all came from that first leadership election four years ago. It had inspired Ali Milani. It had inspired Faiza Shaheen, Zarah Sultana and Bell Ribeiro-Addy. A new generation of political leaders. A new politics.

★ ★ ★

The morning after the election was announced, I was at Norrette's house to work through our plan for the coming weeks. Away from the campaigning part of the campaign were the technical elements of getting my name on the ballot, following election laws and ensuring no one went to prison – the stuff Norrette was amazing at, and the stuff I just sucked at.

We spoke through my nominators, a required list of people who sponsored a particular candidate on the ballot. All candidates were required to have these. We decided against some of our core campaigners, including on this list former Conservative voters who had switched their allegiance to us, those who were ignoring party preference to vote for a local, full-time MP, as opposed to someone who was merely using the constituency as a stepping stone in their political careers.

We agreed the financing, timetable and all other details of the next few weeks. I say agreed – Norrette had done all the work and I just nodded along. I trusted Norrette with my life and knew that she would get it right. I was also itching to get out and campaign. I practically had one hand on the doorknob most of the morning. The starting gun had been fired, I thought – I should be running towards the finish line.

That week we held some of the most extraordinary campaign sessions of the election race. The campaign had the buzz of a carnival or a festival – morning, afternoon and evening rallies and canvassing sessions featuring thousands of people. Volunteers travelling from all across the country and spending their entire weekdays and weekends knocking on doors in Uxbridge and South Ruislip.

That Thursday evening, I arrived at a scheduled canvassing session in a car park in Cavendish ward in the north of our constituency. Having completed the day's media interviews, we were ready to go back out. The only problem was, we had run out of doors to knock on. As I sat at the boot of my car, chatting away with volunteers who had arrived early, James, our campaign manager coordinator, approached to let me know that we'd had so many campaigners arriving for the morning and afternoon sessions that we had no more canvassing sheets to complete (sheets were groups of roads we would canvass at a time) this evening.

As the sun set, more and more volunteers trickled into the car park, and the only thing lighting our crowd became the dim lamps and car headlights. We called Andy to drive some more sheets our way. When Andy arrived, he told us that the entire ward had been done – there were no more doors to knock on. 'That's alright' I said, 'I'll just thank everyone for coming out and send them home early, we could all use an evening off.'

As we gathered the crowd, James and I told them we appreciated the incredible support but we had knocked on every door and so everybody could go home for the evening and rejoin us the following morning. The response was not what we expected: 'No.'

They wouldn't go home. The volunteers had collectively decided that there was no time for an evening off, that they were here and willing to fight. 'We'll knock the doors again, if that's okay? We'll hand out more leaflets. We can stand by the train station as people come home.'

James, Andy and I huddled at the boot of Andy's car and couldn't contain some laughter. How had we come to this? From days where we had had to beg for one or two volunteers in Hillingdon East (a target ward) to volunteers refusing to go home in Cavendish (a Conservative strong ward). The power of belief. Of dreams. This campaign wasn't just about us anymore; it was about their dreams for a better country and for a better world. And tonight, even we were standing in the way of them fighting for it.

As the 'short campaign' (the term used to refer to the six weeks leading up to polling day) got underway and the days passed and turned into weeks, our campaign structure remained the same, but its intensity went right up. More rallies, more leaflets, more stump speeches, more media interviews and more house calls with voters. It was undeniable that the momentum was on our side.

Noises from the Conservative camp began trickling in. They were concerned that the scale of our campaign, combined with a national Labour swing, would be enough to cause the biggest upset in British political history.

They were also looking at the same polling we were. In the second week of the short campaign, I received a call from Ollie Hill. Ollie was an old friend from my days in the student movement and now worked at PeoplesMomentum. He asked if I was with anyone, and I replied that I was just on the doorstep with campaigners. With a calm and gentle voice, he asked me not to react, but told me that polling they had seen had us within the margin of error of beating Boris. 'I think you can pull this off mate.' Labour's Ali Milani on 39 per cent and Conservative's Boris Johnson on 43 per cent. With every poll I saw, my heart beat a little faster. My stomach sank a little deeper. Just imagine the scenes, I thought to myself.

The weeks leading up to polling day were littered with one extraordinary event after another, the sorts of images I would never have imagined myself in. The Labour battle bus came to Uxbridge and we connected our local rally with that of the national Labour campaign. Lord Buckethead, a spoof candidate who literally wore a bucket on his head and followed the prime minister in every election, called me on my personal number to let me know he was endorsing me. 'Thanks, I guess?' I replied, confused as to whether to accept or not. And even Hugh Grant offered to come out and help us campaign.

The rollercoaster was well and truly on its final swings, and it wasn't coming to an end without some final twists and turns.

But the thing I was most excited by was the debate. All throughout this journey, I had said to those around me that at the very least, I would get to debate Boris Johnson at some point. I believed that that alone would be worth the price of running in this race. I could finally look him in the eye and tell him the damage he'd caused our communities and our country, the nasty form of divisive politics he had unleashed in the UK. How his lazy and racist language had correlated to a sharp rise in hate crime and racism. It would be my chance to hold him to account on behalf of the whole country.

We had done our homework. Looking at previous elections in Uxbridge and South Ruislip, we could see Boris would show up to at least one of the locally organised debates in the constituency. In the two election cycles he had run in Uxbridge, he had always attended at least one of the public debates. The previous election it had been the hustings in Yiewsley, and so our assumption was it would be there again. And that is what I prepared for.

In the lead-up to the Yiewsley debate, I spent all my lunch breaks and time between engagements vociferously writing notes to prepare for the debate. I kept a mini booklet with me, to jot down any stories, lines or policies that came to mind. It is something I had become used to in political life. I knew lines for speeches or press interviews might come to me while sat in a waiting room or on a bus, and I always needed a medium to jot them down on.

It was entirely possible that in this general election, Boris would refuse to debate the leader of the Labour Party on national TV, as his predecessors had done, and so our whole team knew that this may well be a unique opportunity. It may turn out that I, alone, would be the only Labour person directly debating the prime minister in the lead-up to polling day.

But it would be an unfulfilled dream. It was a cold November day when I walked towards the Yiewsley hustings. As I approached the venue, I could see the commotion outside the small church that was to be our host for the evening. A familiar sight – bright lights, cameras, a huddle of journalists and activists.

Inside was bitter disappointment. As I completed a few quick 'pre-game' interviews at the door, I could sense the disappointment as I stepped into the room. It had a low-key, theatre-style set-up, with around 100 chairs for local constituent audience members. At the front was a table with name place cards of all the major candidates. In the centre was 'Boris Johnson' and directly to his left (ironically) was 'Ali Milani'. Game time, I thought. But the faces in the room told a different story.

Quite quickly after arriving, the event organiser broke the news to me – Boris Johnson was not coming. For the first time since standing in Uxbridge and South Ruislip, he was not going to attend a hustings and debate his opponent in front of constituents. I was angry, disappointed and frustrated, all at the same time. At first, I felt angry as a candidate. All those hours of preparation we had done, all that time developing messages that we knew would not only connect here in Uxbridge, but around the country too. All gone to waste.

Quickly, my anger turned from candidate to constituent. I lived here, too, and by refusing to even show up, Boris had disrespected all of us. Were we not worth an evening to him? Did he have something to hide? Did he really hold his own constituents in such contempt, that even the simplest of political traditions was not to be respected?

The answer is, of course, in the whole Boris Johnson story. He was treating Uxbridge and South Ruislip the same way he had treated everyone else in his political life: as a stepping stone. We were a means to an end. He had no connection to this area, no love for its communities, and so this was a natural chapter in the story of Boris Johnson and Uxbridge and South Ruislip.

Our task became clearer on this dark, cold November night. We had to put an end to his story in Uxbridge and South Ruislip.

* * *

Thursday, 12 December 2019 came in a flash.

After over 15 months of relentless campaigning, we had reached maximum momentum. Every rally and campaign event packed. Every news cycle a mention of our story. Polling day was going to be the crescendo of our journey. It was the day we would have the audacity to dream of changing our politics forever.

Naturally, the night before brought me no sleep. My tiny studio apartment was stuffed with friends and former colleagues who had travelled from around the country to help. As I stared at the ceiling and the seconds turned to minutes and to hours, the onslaught of anxiety would not let me sleep.

Over and over in my head, I pictured being stood on the stage next to the prime minister as the returning officer read the results. I pictured every scenario. Victory and jubilation. Defeat and embarrassment. My shoulders felt heavier than they had at any point in the campaign that night. I knew how much everyone had sacrificed for me – James, and Andy, and Jane, and Norrette, and Tim, and Ray, and so many more. They deserved this. I looked down at the floor, to a row of people asleep, from the front door all the way to the kitchen, all of whom had given up work and family to help.

I desperately did not want to let any of them down.

The day began at 5am. Without a wink of sleep, I got out of bed and began waking the rest of the team up. As they all rose from their short-lived slumber and began to get ready to head out for what promised to be a long, and potentially historic, day, I noticed something. The people in the room were, for the most part, the same as those I had had the first meeting with late in the spring of 2018. That day we discussed the *idea* of running against Boris; today we would actually be doing it.

First, we headed towards our two campaign headquarters. Our team had hired out two centrally located halls in the constituency for volunteers to base the polling day campaign out of. The first was a Quakers hall in central Uxbridge, a small building that sat at the end of a little public garden, giving it some peace and quiet from the main road. The second location was a hall on the second floor of a local rugby team just off the motorway exit in South Ruislip. The Quakers hall would service the five wards in the south and the rugby hall the three wards in the north.

Polling day campaigning is remarkably straightforward. Having spent over a year knocking on doors around the constituency and asking people how they intended to vote, election day itself focuses on only one thing: getting your vote out. Throughout the year, every single voter who had told us they were voting Labour would have been marked in our internal database. On polling day, that database prints us out sheets, ward by ward, marking where all our votes are. From the moment polls open to the second they close, our army of volunteers knock on doors and phone everyone who told us they would be supporting us, and encourage them to get out and vote.

Two weeks or so from Christmas, it was no surprise that election day was desperately cold. A winter election was already bound to benefit the Conservatives. Every indication had historically told us that a lower turnout would benefit Boris Johnson, and an election in the middle of winter, with the cold, rain and early sunset, indicated a lower turnout than usual. This was, of course, part of the plan of setting an election only weeks away from Christmas Day.

As I sat in our campaign HQ, just as the sun was rising, I reflected on how far we had come. From a campaign figuring it out as we went along, to an election day operation that rivalled a US presidential caucus. Our campaign HQ had been sectioned into five different areas, each representing a different ward, each with one member of our core campaign team supervising its turnout operation. This meant that at any given moment in the day, we would know exactly how turnout looked among our supporters in any ward in the constituency. We also had a separate break room, a kitchen for volunteers to prepare teas and coffees, and we even had a 'Labour mini-cab' service where volunteer drivers would support people needing to get to and from the polling stations. It was clear to me, even at the crack of dawn on 12 December, that we were not going to lose this election through any fault of organisation.

The first volunteers walked through the door at 6am. Almost as if guided by fate, they came through the door singing

Christmas carols and dressed in Santa Claus outfits. Having travelled over four hours from Liverpool through the night, they reassured me at that moment that we were certainly not going to have a shortage of volunteers.

After completing a round of morning interviews just outside our campaign HQ – ending with a live one-on-one with CNN – I walked back into our volunteer base to see our campaign operating seamlessly. Hundreds of volunteers were coming in, being organised, trained and sent out to knock on doors and to get our vote out. We were in gear and we set out for the most important day of my life.

The adrenaline of election day had kicked in for most of us, and we campaigned non-stop. Dropping reminder leaflets in South Ruislip, knocking on doors in Uxbridge South, speaking to commuters outside railway stations and occasionally stopping off for our round of press interviews, I could feel the energy of the campaign we had all built over the previous 15 months. The hours in the day were passing rapidly.

Around midday I was called back into Uxbridge HQ to give a speech to a growing crowd of volunteers on their lunch breaks. We had been joined by Owen Jones and Ash Sarkar, and it was our opportunity to both thank and motivate our activists. As we parked up, I could see this small Quakers hall was completely overtaken by Labour activists, hundreds of volunteers spilling out into the garden, out of the front doors. And they all looked familiar. Young faces, people of colour, folks who had never believed in politics because politics had never given a damn about them.

As we squeezed into the main hall, we each took it in turns to stand on a chair and give a rallying call to the hundreds of activists who had given up their day (many of them weeks and even months) to campaign alongside us. Owen spoke of what might be possible if Labour were to come into power; Ash described the relief of defeating Boris; and I, as I had done for the whole campaign, told my story:

> Today we can do something remarkable. Something
> so many – mostly in the press and political
> establishment – have been telling me is not possible.

We can send shockwaves through Westminster and politics all around the world. Just imagine, turning on your TV tonight and hearing that we have a Labour government ... that Boris Johnson is no longer Prime Minister ... and that his own seat of Uxbridge and South Ruislip is a Labour gain!

And then imagine if the person who beats him is a young kid who came to this country as an immigrant at five years old, grew up in a council estate with a single parent, went to comprehensive school and came up right through the community. Imagine what that would say about our politics, about our country.

So here's what we are going to do. We are going to go out, we are going to knock on doors, we are going to talk to voters and we are going to make sure, in just nine hours, we change the world together!

I felt the room erupt, not just with noise, but also with hope. With belief. Hundreds of people, in one place, with one dream, working together to make it reality.

Unfortunately, this was also the moment I first got a sense that something was going very wrong.

As I stepped off the chair, took a few selfies and made my way to the office in the back to catch my breath, I caught a glimpse of Andy. Andy was in charge of running the whole Uxbridge polling operation, and so my first thought was to ask him how things were looking. 'It's going okay, don't you worry about the numbers mate', he replied instinctually. He placed his arm on my shoulder, 'You just focus on getting out and talking to voters.' That was not good. I had worked with Andy long enough to know he was not satisfied with the numbers he was seeing come back from our key wards. 'It's okay' is not the response of someone who is optimistic about prospects.

So I snuck into one of our key wards to look at the sheets coming back from our target areas. I saw what Andy had been seeing all day. Labour supporters across the ward who had told us they were supporting us were, in the last moment, breaking away from us. My heart dropped. I could see the same word scribbled in different-coloured pens and different handwriting across different sheets: 'Brexit', 'Brexit', 'Fucking Brexit'.

From this moment, and as I headed into marginal territory, I could sense the election getting away from us. Too many supporters we were relying on were changing their votes at the last minute. Some even apologised on the doorstep, saying they desperately didn't want to do it, but they felt like our national Brexit positioning was preventing them from supporting us.

As the sun set, I found myself with a small team by Brunel University. It was rather apropos to be canvassing adjacent to where my political story had started. As we made our way along the road, I got to a door I recognised. Speaking to a small family of four, whom I had spent some time with a few weeks prior and had convinced to vote Labour, I asked if they had been out to vote yet. The dad said they had. From the look on his face I knew we had lost their vote. 'You didn't, did you?' I asked, more in hope than expectation. 'I'm really sorry, Ali, we just can't take another four years of Brexit conversation dominating our lives.' This wasn't even a Leave voting family; it was purely fatigue.

As I walked back to my team, it started to rain. Huddled under a single umbrella, as our sheets became soaked, I knew we were done. In that very moment, I knew we had lost. I turned to my brother-in-law, Mojtaba, who had been by my side most of the day for security, and told him in Farsi, 'I think this has gotten away from us.'

We continued for the next four hours, alongside an army of volunteers, to blitz through the entire constituency. Every voter who had indicated their support for us got two, sometimes three knocks on the door, reminding them to vote. Our campaign HQs in Uxbridge and South Ruislip had thousands of volunteers from across the globe come through and fight alongside us.

I knew we had truly sparked fear into Boris's team when, just as polls were about to close, I was shown a picture by Mohammed Bux of Boris Johnson himself leafleting in the north of constituency. 'You have the prime minister panic campaigning in his own seat with 20 minutes to go.' Well, I guess that's something, I thought.

We made our way back to the Quakers hall as polls closed. I could feel, in the final hour, the nerves begin to really ramp up, like a ball of barbed wire in my stomach, slowly getting bigger and bigger. I knew the exit polls would absolutely confirm whether we had a shot at winning or if we were headed towards defeat. The exit polls in UK elections tended to be very accurate and gave a strong indication of which way individual seats would go.

As we approached 10pm, the main hall came to a sudden silence. As I stood, arms crossed, in front of the TV screen, waiting for my future, Andy came across and put his arms around me. A comforting moment, letting me know that whatever the result, we would be going through it together. The clock struck 10, and Huw Edwards announced the exit poll results. 'Our exit poll is suggesting that there will be a Conservative majority when all the votes are counted to this election of December 2019. The Conservatives on 368 seats, Labour way down on 191.'

Defeat.

It felt like a bullet to the chest. I felt my heart sink and my shoulders dropped down towards the earth. It was the first time in my life I had ever felt such disappointment, such devastation. Feeling my throat begin to tense up, I became very aware that I was in a very public place and I decided to head to the back room that had been set up for me to wait in as they counted our votes. I sat in that room a while, with Mojtaba and a few friends who had been asked to keep me company in the hours between polls closing and the results being officially declared. We sat in silence.

Omar Al Roubaie, a friend from school, asked if there was any chance we could win based on that exit poll. 'No chance' I replied. Labour were getting hammered nationally, and there was no way on that much of a national voter swing away from Labour that I could win in the prime minister's own constituency.

I sat there for an hour staring at the floor. Replaying the election over in my head. Wondering if all of this had been worth it. The death threats, my name and future job prospects dragged through every national paper, the financial insecurity and so much more. That feeling was immediately followed by a wave of guilt. This was not about me. The tragedy was what was going to happen to our working-class communities. All those people I had told we would be bringing change. They would have another five years of Tory rule, another five years of Boris Johnson.

As all these thoughts rattled in my shell-shocked mind, Andy came into our back office. 'I know you aren't going to want to hear this, mate, but the volunteers won't leave without hearing from you first.' For the second time in this election, our people were refusing to leave. They wanted to hear from the candidate in whom they had placed their hopes, of what would happen next.

It was the hardest speech I have ever had to deliver. To inject some hope, some optimism, in a moment of defeat. To try and lift people up when I, myself, was at the lowest I have ever been. I took one breath and went outside. Seeing the hundred or so people crammed into the garden outside the Quakers hall brought a tear to my eye. They deserved victory, not defeat. They deserved everything.

I don't remember what I said. I was too emotionally vulnerable to have choreographed a coherent speech. But I spoke from the heart and remembered how it ended: 'And let me tell you this, I would rather lose with each and every one of you, than win with Boris Johnson.'

★ ★ ★

Mercifully, the latter part of election night went by rather quickly. Within a few hours it was clear that Labour had lost all bar one of its marginal constituencies around the country, and before we knew it we had been summoned to Brunel University for the results. Norrette and I were taken to the back with Boris Johnson and his team and were walked through the results. Boris Johnson had received 25,351 votes and Ali Milani 18,141. I was surprised by those numbers. They were higher for us than I had expected, given the national picture. But what I remember most is Boris's erratic behaviour in the room. He was clearly jovial at the results, as one would expect, but it went beyond the spirits of a victor. It was almost like a child having won first prize at the local fair. On more than one occasion he had to be calmed by his entourage. I also remember him refusing to acknowledge me after the results had been read.

It wasn't long before we were taken on stage, for a live broadcast for the world to see, as the results were read out. We both spoke – Boris Johnson set out his stall and government for the next five years, and I thanked my team and volunteers for all they had done, and reminded all who were dejected that this was not the end of our fight. It must have gone well because even local Tories approached me after the speech to compliment its tone.

It took a few months for me to really crunch the numbers and to see that, even in defeat, something special had happened for us in Uxbridge and South Ruislip. While Labour had been hammered around the country, with one of the worst results since 1939, in the prime minister's own seat we had outperformed nearly every other Labour marginal seat in the country. While Labour's national swing was –8 per cent, our performance had only recorded a net 2 per cent drop off – outperforming the national party by over 6 per cent. This made us one of the best performing seats in the UK. We had recorded nearly the same 18,000 votes that had been achieved at the height of the election over performance in 2017, even though in 2017 Labour had a swing of 10 per cent in favour and in 2019 an 8 per cent swing against.

This had also been done in the prime minister's own constituency where, traditionally, there is a prime minister's bounce. One of the things we had been quietly worried about in the campaign was this bounce. This would be a lift in the votes of the prime minister in their own seat as, generally, voters enjoyed the fact that their local MP was also the prime minister. History shows us this is very much the case. In 2010, David Cameron's prime minister bounce saw an increase of 9.4 per cent[8] in his constituency. Gordon Brown also saw a bounce of 6.4 per cent in 2010, and Tony Blair a bounce of 10.7 per cent in 1997.[9] In Uxbridge and South Ruislip, in the midst of a hammering of Labour nationally, we kept Boris's bounce down to just 1.8 per cent.

All the data suggested that even in defeat, electorally we had accomplished something impressive in Uxbridge and South Ruislip. But ultimately, I knew none of it mattered. Whether we lost by one vote or 10,000, the outcome was one and the same: a loss. We would not be able to bring about the change I so desperately wanted for our communities.

I didn't get back home until 5am the next morning. As I climbed into bed, I felt like my worst fears had come true. I had let everybody down. I was embarrassed, angry, and, more than anything, worried about the future. After everything I had learned about the man who is Boris Johnson, I feared his premiership marked dangerous things for working-class communities, for minorities, for women, for all of us.

I got up later that morning to find an empty fridge. I had hardly spent a minute in the flat for the previous three months, and naturally, the fridge was empty. As I walked towards the local off-licence, I could sense my life was different now. It no longer had the urgency of a campaign, the hanging anxiety of polling day.

As I walked into the store and received a sympathetic nod from the owner, I made my way to the fridge for a pint of milk. Just then, a large, middle-aged man walked towards me. 'Are you Ali Milani?' he asked. 'Yes sir' I replied. 'Ali Milani as in the Labour guy?' 'Yep, that would be me.' He looked at me a while, shook his head before staring dead into my eyes and saying: 'Labour's shit.'

Well, I guess that's one way to get reintroduced back into the real world.

Epilogue

It had been a long and difficult journey.

What began in the spring of 2018 as just a silly idea, one that I had laughed away, had ended in 2019 on a stage, shoulder to shoulder with Prime Minister Boris Johnson. It had been a long and gruelling road, but one filled with lessons for our future – lessons for me as an individual, and also reflections for our politics as a whole. As the immediacy and pain of the result has passed in the months since that cold December night, I have been able to see more clearly the real lessons of this whole campaign.

Throughout the 15-month campaign I had thought it was the result of this election that determined the state of our politics. I believed that it was only in victory that we could point to this story as an example of what is possible in modern British politics.

But I was wrong.

It was never the result, but the journey that made this story special. The lessons weren't in the destination, but rather the road that got us to where we were. Every twist, every obstacle and every wall we hit along the way brought with it a fundamental lesson for the future. I was never supposed to be an MP. This political system, both in the Labour Party and beyond, was not built for a 24-year-old, working-class, Muslim immigrant to take on the prime minister. But we did. We built a campaign that broke so many of the 'traditional' rules. From the global media coverage to the thousands upon thousands of volunteers from across the world, we came closer to defeating a prime minister than anyone has in nearly 100 years. And it was in that journey that we saw something very few others have – we saw the heart of the country.

I have written this book and told my story because, although the challenges we faced along the way were vast, I want everyone reading it to know that in facing them I have become more hopeful than ever. In meeting the people, fighting alongside them and having the honour of representing them on that stage, I have found that hope that is in such short supply. I was more optimistic about politics the day after I had lost the election than the day before.

I believe buried in my story is a reason for all those like me to believe that they have a place in politics. There are a million examples as to why.

From early on, we saw the inherent inaccessibility and flaws in the Labour Party primary process. Yet, despite what seemed like insurmountable odds, the Uxbridge and South Ruislip Labour Party chose to select a young, Muslim, immigrant as their candidate against Boris Johnson. They put their faith in me, when a safer choice must have seemed so much more appealing. They believed, maybe even before I did.

The levels of institutional racism in our politics and our society are vast. I faced them every day as a candidate, from biased media coverage to death threats delivered to my door. On so many occasions, I felt I did not belong and would never be expected to win. But as I knocked on door after door, and spoke to family after family, I saw a community that was not only willing to embrace me, but who also more closely resembled my life and my story than that of a certain Boris Johnson, a community that had been failed by leaders unwilling to talk about immigration and race with conviction. That was our job now.

There were also the financial barriers that placed so much pressure on me and my family, barriers that no doubt continue to prevent thousands of good public servants in waiting. Yet, at a time when we needed it most, we saw a community willing to give the little they had for a better world. Working-class members and families, who themselves struggled day to day to make ends meet, giving £5, £10, to change the nature of our politics – because they trusted in us and wanted to change our politics.

The nature of our national media was perhaps the biggest challenge we faced. Headlines and reports of half-truths, mistruths and biased coverage. Yet even within that enormous world, there were journalists willing to tell our story honestly, who would hold us to account fairly and cover our journey accurately. There was also a community that was smarter than I had expected, who knew to look at some of the (far right) press for what it is: a vehicle of division. They wanted to help us build something better.

These are but a few examples. There are thousands more buried in the chapters of this story and in the living examples of others in our politics. Yes, they may be few in number, and politics often gives us an infinite number of reasons to lose hope and faith. But my story has taught me that there are equal numbers of reasons to be hopeful, to believe. Reasons to fight on.

This campaign was anything but a smooth ride, and I have tried my best to lay out the real challenges we faced along the way in as honest a way as possible. But more than all of these things, I honestly believe my unlikely candidacy and this entire story has shown us that the country is ready for something different. Through the voices of voters in our community and the faces of the thousands of people who travelled across countries and continents to fight alongside us, we saw people waiting for something different. Here in the UK and around the world, they are waiting for political leaders to inspire them into a new generation for our politics, leaders who have the basic strength to drive us into a new era, leaders who have the courage to tackle the questions of our time.

Those leaders are out there. But if there is one thing this story, my story, has shown, it is that they won't be found in the same old places we have always looked. They are not in the common rooms of Eton, Oxford or Cambridge. They aren't in the tea rooms of the House of Lords. They are in our communities. They are reading this book right now. They are you.

I must have found a million excuses not to do it. I was too young. Too inexperienced. No one would take me seriously.

But I did it anyway. And I am damn glad I did.

Notes

Chapter 1

1   The Public Whip (2010) 'University tuition fee gap – Raise upper limit to £9,000 per year', 9 December (www.publicwhip.org.uk/division. php?date=2010-12-09&number=150).

2   The Sutton Trust and Social Mobility Commission (2019) *Elitist Britain 2019: The educational backgrounds of Britain's leading people*, London (https:// assets.publishing.service.gov.uk/government/uploads/system/uploads/ attachment_data/file/811045/Elitist_Britain_2019.pdf).

3   See www.votesat16.org/about/campaign-history

4   Stephan Mashford (2020) 'Youth turnout – How does the UK compare to other European nations?', 89 Scotland, 28 September (https://89initiative. com/youth-turnout-uk-europe).

5   Jason Cowley (2018) 'Who is the real John McDonnell', *The New Statesman*, 5 September (www.newstatesman.com/uncategorized/2018/09/who-real-john-mcdonnell).

Chapter 2

1   https://twitter.com/Keir_Starmer/status/1224662165271056385

2   Labour Party (2019) *Rule book 2019*, London (https://labour.org.uk/wp-content/uploads/2019/04/Rule-Book-2019.pdf), pp 32, 33.

3   Rhys Williams (2011) *What works in candidate selection?*, London: Institute for Government (www.instituteforgovernment.org.uk/sites/default/files/ publications/What%20works%20in%20candidate%20selection.pdf).

4   Williams (2011) *What works in candidate selection?*, pp 4, 5.

5   Williams (2011) *What works in candidate selection?*, pp 4, 5.

6   Jean-Benoît Pilet, Rumyana Kolarova, Vladimir Shopov, Mats Braun, Vít Beneš, Jan Karlas et al (2009) *The selection of candidates for the European Parliament by national parties and the impact of European political parties*, Brussels: European Parliament (www.europarl.europa.eu/RegData/etudes/etudes/ join/2009/410683/IPOL-AFCO_ET(2009)410683_EN.pdf), p 351.

7   BBC News (2021) 'Liverpool mayoral election: Labour reveals new candidates', 2 March (www.bbc.co.uk/news/uk-england-merseyside -56257787).

8   Sienna Rodgers (2021) 'Labour suspends Liverpool mayor candidate selection race', LabourList, 17 February (https://labourlist.org/2021/02/ labour-suspends-liverpool-mayor-candidate-selection-race).

9 See www.washingtonpost.com/politics/2019/11/15/how-run-congress/
   ?arc404=true
10 Pilet et al (2009) *The selection of candidates*, p 62.
11 Pilet et al (2009) *The selection of candidates*, pp 47, 48.

Chapter 3

1 R. Kelly Garrett (2019) 'Social media's contribution to political
   misperceptions in US presidential elections', *PLoS ONE*, 14(3), e0213500
   (https://doi.org/10.1371/journal.pone.0213500).
2 Edelman Research (2009) 'The social pulpit: Barack Obama's social
   media toolkit' (www.mediadb.eu/fileadmin/downloads/reports/Edelman_
   Digital_Public_Affairs.pdf), p. 1.
3 Jennifer Aaker and Victoria Chang (2009) *Obama and the power of social media
   and technology*, Stanford, CA: Stanford Graduate School of Business, p 2.
4 Jose Antonio Vargas (2008) 'Obama raised half a billion online', *The
   Washington Post*, 20 November.
5 Rahaf Harfoush (2008) 'Inside the Obama campaign: Lessons learned',
   equilateral quadrilateral, 8 December (www.happywookie.wordpress.
   com/2008/12/08/102).
6 The quote is from Aaker and Chang (2009) *Obama and the power of social
   media*, p 2.
7 Garrett (2019) 'Social media's contribution'.
8 Leocadia Diáz Romero (2014) 'On the web and contemporary social
   movements', in Bogdan Pătruț and Monica Pătruț (eds) *Social media in
   politics: Case studies on the political power of social media*, Cham: Springer, p 23.
9 Romero (2014) 'On the web', p 31.
10 Romero (2014) 'On the web', p 31.
11 Tim Highfield (2016) *Social media and everyday politics*, Cambridge: Polity.
12 Highfield (2016) *Social media*.
13 Richard Seymour (2019) *The twittering machine*, London: The Indigo Press,
   p 29.
14 Seymour (2019) *The twittering machine*, p 29.
15 Ilyas Nagdee (2019) 'We all say things we regret. Trawling young activists'
   tweets denies them a chance', *The Guardian*, 19 November (www.the
   guardian.com/commentisfree/2019/nov/19/trawling-social-media-
   tweets-politics-student-union).
16 Ali Milani (2018) 'In 2017, student politics needs to grow up', *HuffPost*,
   5 January (www.huffingtonpost.co.uk/ali-milani/2017-student-politics
   _b_13935992.html).
17 Greg Barradale (2017) 'NUS officials call for Ali Milani to withdraw
   after he tweeted that Jews are stingy', The Tab (https://thetab.com/
   uk/2017/04/12/nus-officials-call-ali-milani-withdraw-tweeted-jews-
   stingy-37560).
18 Frances Corry (2021) 'Screenshot, save, share, shame: Making sense of new
   media through screenshots and public shame', *First Monday*, 26(4), 5 April
   (https://firstmonday.org/ojs/index.php/fm/article/view/11649/10107).

19 Zamzam Ibrahim (2017) 'The tabloids published my teenage tweets and implied I'm a fanatical Muslim – so let me set the record straight', *Independent*, 3 July (www.independent.co.uk/voices/fanatical-muslim-tweets-islam-zamzam-ibrahim-student-politics-truth-a7821591.html).

20 Ben Beaumont-Thomas (2017) 'Stormzy apologises for unearthed homophobic tweets', *The Guardian*, 22 November (www.theguardian.com/music/2017/nov/22/stormzy-apologises-for-unearthed-homophobic-tweets).

21 Seymour (2019) *The twittering machine*, p 83.

22 Seymour (2019) *The twittering machine*, p 39.

23 Nazia Parveen (2020) 'New Tory MP pictured with alleged far-right activists', *The Guardian*, 14 February (www.theguardian.com/politics/2020/feb/14/dehenna-davison-new-tory-mp-pictured-with-alleged-far-right-activists).

24 Milani (2018) 'In 2017, student politics needs to grow up'.

25 Nagdee (2019) 'We all say things we regret'.

26 Nagdee (2019) 'We all say things we regret'.

Chapter 4

1 UNESCO, Samarra Archaeological City (https://whc.unesco.org/en/list/276).

2 Fox News (2003) 'Firefights leave dozens of Iraqis dead', 2 December (www.foxnews.com/story/firefights-leave-dozens-of-iraqis-dead).

3 Dexter Filkins and Ian Fisher (2003) 'US sees lesson for insurgents in an Iraqi battle', *The New York Times*, 2 December (www.nytimes.com/2003/12/02/world/us-sees-lesson-for-insurgents-in-an-iraq-battle.html).

4 Aljazeera (2003) 'Samarra clash toll still a mystery', 2 December (www.aljazeera.com/news/2003/12/2/samarra-clash-toll-still-a-mystery).

5 Matthew Gentzkow and Jesse M. Shapiro (2006) 'Media bias and reputation', *Journal of Political Economy*, 114(2) (www.brown.edu/Research/Shapiro/pdfs/bias.pdf), p 281.

6 www.youtube.com/watch?v=uO8jOmJ70nM&t=135s

7 https://twitter.com/TaheraKhan20/status/1112835921253154816

8 Kryi Evangelou, Maeve Shearlaw and Katie Lamborn (2019) 'Will this young Muslim be Boris Johnson's ultimate downfall? – video', *The Guardian*, 27 June (www.theguardian.com/politics/video/2019/jun/27/will-this-young-muslim-be-boris-johnsons-ultimate-downfall-video).

9 https://twitter.com/davidlammy/status/1148525971873681408?s=21

10 https://twitter.com/okwonga/status/1146414867114528769?s=21

11 www.youtube.com/watch?v=F8wKRg-1e6s

12 According to the Media Reform Coalition (www.mediareform.org.uk).

13 William Shawcross (1999) 'Rupert Murdoch', *Time*, 3 November (https://web.archive.org/web/20060618211609/http://www.time.com/time/magazine/intl/article/0%2C9171%2C1107991025-33716%2C00.html).

14 Andy McSmith (2012) 'Revealed: Murdoch's secret meeting with Mrs Thatcher before he bought The Times', *Independent*, 17 March

(www.independent.co.uk/news/media/press/revealed-murdoch-s-secret-meeting-with-mrs-thatcher-before-he-bought-the-times-7575910.html).

15 Jane Martinson (2016) 'Rupert Murdoch describes Brexit as "wonderful"', *The Guardian*, 28 June (www.theguardian.com/media/2016/jun/28/rupert-murdoch-brexit-wonderful-donald-trump).

16 Martinson (2016) 'Rupert Murdoch'.

17 David Folkenflik (2017) 'Murdoch and Trump, an alliance of mutual interest', NPR, 14 March (www.npr.org/sections/thetwo-way/2017/03/14/520080606/murdoch-and-trump-an-alliance-of-mutual-interest?t=1629555634207).

18 Max Chalmers (2015) 'Rupert Murdoch has "more impact than any living Australian" says Tony Abbott', New Matilda, 13 November (https://newmatilda.com/2015/11/13/rupert-murdoch-has-more-impact-than-any-living-australian-says-tony-abbott).

19 Catherine Vervier (2008) 'The end of the affair: Dacre moves towards Cameron', *Independent*, 20 July (www.independent.co.uk/news/media/the-end-of-the-affair-dacre-moves-towards-cameron-872278.html).

20 Michael White (2006) 'Cash for peerages? What's new in that?', *PRWeek*, 20 April (www.prweek.com/article/554399/michael-white-cash-peerages-whats-new-that).

21 Media Reform Coalition (2019) *Who owns the UK media?* (www.mediareform.org.uk/wp-content/uploads/2019/03/FINALonline2.pdf).

22 Curtis Howard (2019) 'Reforming the British press', *The Social Review*, 23 July (www.thesocialreview.co.uk/2019/07/23/reforming-the-british-press).

23 Media Reform Coalition (2019) *Who owns the UK media?*

24 Atkins (2016) *Skewed: A critical thinkers guide to media bias*, Amherst, NY: Prometheus Books, p 9.

25 Atkins (2016) *Skewed*, p 20.

26 Gentzkow and Shapiro (2006) 'Media bias', p 282.

27 Gentzkow and Shapiro (2006) 'Media bias', p 282.

28 Gentzkow and Shapiro (2006) 'Media bias', p 282.

29 Martin Fletcher (2021) 'Why the Foxification of the British media must be resisted', *The New Statesman*, 18 January (www.newstatesman.com/politics/media/2021/01/why-foxification-british-media-must-be-resisted).

30 Rowena Mason (2020) 'Dominic Cummings thinktank called for "end of BBC in current form"', *The Guardian*, 21 January (www.theguardian.com/politics/2020/jan/21/dominic-cummings-thinktank-called-for-end-of-bbc-in-current-form).

31 Fletcher (2021) 'Why the Foxification of the British media ...'.

32 Archie Bland (2021) 'Rishi Sunak's adviser Richard Sharp to be next BBC chair', *The Guardian*, 6 January (www.theguardian.com/media/2021/jan/06/former-goldman-sachs-banker-richard-sharp-to-be-next-bbc-chairman).

33 Michael Minors, Dennis Grenham and Lovedeep Vaid (1994) *London borough council by-elections, May 1990 to May 1994*, London: London

Research Centre (https://londondatastore-upload.s3.amazonaws.com/docs/LBCBE_1990-5_TO_1994-5.pdf).

34 Mark Sweney (2020) 'BBC appoints insider Tim Davie as director general', *The Guardian*, 5 June (www.theguardian.com/media/2020/jun/05/bbc-appoints-insider-tim-davie-as-director-general).

35 Henry Dyer (2021) 'BBC director who said appointment of ex-HuffPost editor to news role was too political didn't declare his job at Conservative lobbying group', *Insider*, 22 August (www.businessinsider.com/bbc-director-sir-robbie-gibb-didnt-declare-links-tory-lobbyists-2021-8?amp&r=US&IR=T&__twitter_impression=true).

36 Owen Jones (2014) 'It's the BBC's rightwing bias that is the threat to democracy and journalism', *The Guardian*, 17 March (www.theguardian.com/commentisfree/2014/mar/17/bbc-leftwing-bias-non-existent-myth).

37 Jones (2014) 'It's the BBC's rightwing bias'.

38 Mike Berry (2013) 'Hard evidence: How biased is the BBC?', *The New Statesman*, 23 August.

39 Peter Oborne (2019) 'In its election coverage, the BBC has let down the people who believe in it', *The Guardian*, 3 December (www.theguardian.com/commentisfree/2019/dec/03/election-coverage-bbc-tories).

40 Oborne (2019) 'In its election coverage …'.

41 https://twitter.com/bbclaurak/status/1174318249460281346

42 Rowena Mason (2019) 'Two former Labour MPs urge voters to back Boris Johnson', *The Guardian*, 7 November (www.theguardian.com/politics/2019/nov/07/former-labour-mp-ian-austin-urges-voters-back-boris-johnson).

43 Oborne (2019) 'In its election coverage'.

44 Fletcher (2021) 'Why the Foxification of the British media …'.

45 www.youtube.com/watch?v=ZKLRmVYk0-s

46 Media Reform Coalition (2019) *Who owns the UK media?*

47 Sophy Ridge (2019) 'Could a "local working-class kid" unseat Boris Johnson at the next election?', Sky News, 6 October (https://news.sky.com/story/could-a-local-working-class-kid-unseat-boris-johnson-at-the-next-election-11828825).

48 Sheena McKenzie and Anna Stewart (2019) 'It'll take superpowers to unseat Boris Johnson. This comic book fan says he's got them', CNN, 31 August (https://edition.cnn.com/2019/08/30/europe/ali-milani-boris-johnson-uxbridge-gbr-intl/index.html).

49 Ros Wynne Jones (2019) 'Meet the working class Muslim Labour candidate trying to unseat Boris Johnson', *Mirror*, 18 July (www.mirror.co.uk/news/politics/meet-working-class-muslim-labour-18341921).

50 Jen Mills (2019) 'The Muslim immigrant "ready to beat" Boris Johnson at the polls', *Metro*, 17 April (https://metro.co.uk/2019/04/17/muslim-immigrant-ready-beat-boris-johnson-polls-9239152).

51 Anoosh Chakelian (2019) 'Meet Ali Milani, the millennial who could unseat Boris Johnson in Uxbridge', *The New Statesman*, 24 July (www.newstatesman.com/politics/uk/2019/07/meet-ali-milani-millennial-who-could-unseat-boris-johnson-uxbridge).

52 Thomas Colson (2019) 'Boris Johnson could soon become the first sitting prime minister in history to lose his seat', *Business Insider*, 29 September (www.businessinsider.com/boris-johnson-first-prime-minister-to-ever-lose-seat-uxbridge-2019-9?r=US&IR=T).

53 William Wallace (2019) 'Will Boris Johnson lose his seat at the next general election?' *Financial Times*, 28 July (www.ft.com/content/e059eb7a-aed4-11e9-8030-530adfa879c2).

54 Faisal Hanif (2019) *State of media reporting on Islam & Muslims, Quarterly report: Oct–Dec 2018*, London: Centre for Media Monitoring (https://cfmm.org.uk/wp-content/uploads/2019/07/CfMM-Quarterly-Report-Oct-Dec-2018.pdf).

55 Gerard Tubb (2018) *Sky News At Six*, 10 October.

56 Hanif (2019) *State of media reporting*.

57 Hanif (2019) *State of media reporting*.

58 Hanif (2019) *State of media reporting*.

59 Shamim Miah (2015) 'The groomers and the question of race', *Identity Papers: A Journal of British and Irish Studies*, 1(1), p 54 (https://doi.org/10.5920/idp.2015.1154).

60 John Ingham (2009) 'British Muslims are killing our troops', *Express*, 26 February (www.express.co.uk/news/uk/86485/British-Muslims-are-killing-our-troops).

61 Bob Pitt (2010) 'Brit kids forced to eat Halal school dinners, claims outraged Daily Star', Islamophobia Watch, 6 August (http://islamophobiawatch.co.uk/brit-kids-forced-to-eat-halal-school-dinners-claims-outraged-daily-star).

62 John Twomey, David Pilditch and Nathan Rao (2010) 'Muslim plot to kill Pope', *Express*, 18 September (www.express.co.uk/news/uk/200262/Muslim-plot-to-kill-Pope).

63 John Twomey and Cyril Dixon (2010) 'Muslims tell British: Go to hell', *Express*, 4 November (www.express.co.uk/news/uk/209432/Muslims-tell-British-Go-to-hell

64 https://twitter.com/skynews/status/611649538810626050

65 Miah (2015) 'The groomers and the question of race', p 54.

66 Vanessa Allen and Eleanor Harding (2017) 'MPs demand inquiry over five-year-old Christian girl forced to live with Muslim foster carers "who told her Christmas and Easter are stupid and European women are alcoholics"', *Daily Mail*, 28 August (www.dailymail.co.uk/news/article-4831134/MP-anger-Christian-girl-forced-Muslim-foster-care.html).

67 Rod Liddle (2012) 'What the panel thought', *Evening Standard*, 12 April (www.standard.co.uk/hp/front/what-the-panel-thought-6665357.html).

68 Kerry Moore, Paul Mason and Justin Lewis (2008) *Images of Islam in the UK: The Representation of British Muslims in the National Print News Media 2000–2008*, Cardiff: Cardiff School of Journalism, Media and Cultural Studies.

69 Moore et al (2008) *Images of Islam in the UK*.

70 Elizabeth Poole, quoted in Katy Sian, Ian Law and S. Sayyid (2012) *The media and Muslims in the UK*, Leeds: Centre for Ethnicity and Racism

Studies, University of Leeds (https://ces.uc.pt/projectos/tolerace/media/Working%20paper%205/The%20Media%20and%20Muslims%20in%20the%20UK.pdf), p 230.

71 Brittany Vonow (2019) 'Labour activist who wants to unseat Boris Johnson claimed US government was behind 9/11 attack', *The Sun*, 6 November (www.thesun.co.uk/news/10289108/labour-activist-ali-milani-claimed-us-government-behind-911).

72 Matt Dathan (2019) 'Dirty secret: Two wannabe Labour MPs exposed as "supporters of campaign group that praised Jihadi John"', *The Sun*, 18 November (www.thesun.co.uk/news/politics/10369364/labour-mps-exposed-jihadi-john).

73 See https://order-order.com/people/ali-milani

74 Miranda Larbi (2018) 'If we hold minorities up as cultural heroes, the only way for them is down', *Metro*, 23 January (https://metro.co.uk/2018/01/23/hold-minorities-cultural-heroes-way-7252898).

75 Larbi (2018) 'If we hold minorities up as cultural heroes ...'.

76 Ian Birrell (2019) 'Worse than Broadmoor: Nurse whistleblower claims he has seen psychopathic serial killers cared for better than the autistic children he has witnessed being violently held down and force-fed drugs at health unit funded by the NHS', *Mail on Sunday*, 6 January (www.dailymail.co.uk/news/article-6561505/Nurse-says-seen-killers-cared-better-autistic-children-health-unit-funded-NHS.html).

77 Matthew Hickley and Jason Bennetto (2009) 'One out of every five killers is an immigrant', *Mail Online*, 31 August (www.dailymail.co.uk/news/article-1210129/One-killers-immigrant.html).

78 BBC News (2017) 'Daily Mail's "Who won Legs-it!" headline draws scorn, 28 March (www.bbc.co.uk/news/uk-39416554).

79 Lizzie Dearden (2016) 'The Sun and Daily Mail accused of "fuelling prejudice" in report on rising racist violence and hate speech in the UK', *Independent*, 8 October (www.independent.co.uk/news/media/press/the-sun-and-daily-mail-fuelling-prejudice-racist-violence-hate-crime-speech-uk-ecri-report-a7351856.html).

80 Dearden (2016) 'The Sun and Daily Mail'.

Chapter 5

1 Anoosh Chakelian (2019) '"We no longer want the Hollywood show": Meet the 24-year-old Muslim trying to unseat Boris Johnson', *The New Statesman*, 28 January (www.newstatesman.com/politics/uk/2019/01/we-no-longer-want-hollywood-show-meet-24-year-old-muslim-trying-unseat-boris).

2 Remi Joseph Salisbury (2016) 'We can do better than the racist, repugnant, chemical weapon-supporting Churchill on our £5 notes', *Independent*, 13 September (www.independent.co.uk/voices/we-can-do-better-racist-repugnant-chemical-weapon-supporting-churchill-our-ps5-notes-a7245671.html).

3   Stuart Jeffries (2014) 'Britain's most racist election: The story of Smethwick, 50 years on', *The Guardian*, 15 October (www.theguardian.com/world/2014/oct/15/britains-most-racist-election-smethwick-50-years-on).

4   Michael Savage (2018) 'Fifty years on, what is the legacy of Enoch Powell's "rivers of blood" speech?', *The Guardian*, 15 April (www.theguardian.com/world/2018/apr/14/enoch-powell-rivers-blood-legacy-wolverhampton).

5   Gary Younge (2019) 'Given Britain's history it's no surprise that racism still infects our politics', *The Guardian*, 29 November (www.theguardian.com/commentisfree/2019/nov/29/britain-history-racism-infects-politics-slavery-windrush).

6   Rachel Shabi (2019) 'How immigration became Britain's most toxic political issue', *The Guardian*, 15 November (www.theguardian.com/politics/2019/nov/15/how-immigration-became-britains-most-toxic-political-issue).

7   Channel 4 News (2015) 'Net migration figures rise, leaving PM's promise in tatters', 26 February (www.channel4.com/news/net-migration-figures-rise-david-cameron-promise-tatters).

8   Institute for Public Policy Research (2005) 'Asylum in the UK', an ippr FactFile, February (www.ippr.org/files/images/media/files/publication/2011/05/asylum_factfile_feb05_1344.pdf).

9   Quoted in Rachel Shabi (2019) 'How immigration became Britain's most toxic political issue'.

10 See Immigration and Asylum Act, www.legislation.gov.uk/ukpga/1999/33/pdfs/ukpga_19990033_en.pdf

11 Peter Preston (2001) 'The case for ID cards is now overwhelming', *The Guardian*, 1 October (www.theguardian.com/politics/2001/oct/01/Whitehall.humanrights).

12 *The Guardian* (2002) 'Row erupts over Blunkett's "swamped" comment', 24 April (www.theguardian.com/politics/2002/apr/24/immigrationpolicy.immigrationandpublicservices).

13 Erica Consterdine (2018) 'Hostile environment: The UK government's draconian immigration policy explained', *The Conversation*, 26 April (https://theconversation.com/hostile-environment-the-uk-governments-draconian-immigration-policy-explained-95460).

14 Rowena Mason and Frances Perraudin (2016) 'Cameron's "bunch of migrants" jibe is callous and dehumanising, say MPs', *The Guardian*, 27 January (www.theguardian.com/politics/2016/jan/27/david-cameron-bunch-of-migrants-jibe-pmqs-callous-dehumanising).

15 Renae Merle (2018) 'A guide to the financial crisis – 10 years later', *The Washington Post*, 10 September (www.washingtonpost.com/business/economy/a-guide-to-the-financial-crisis--10-years-later/2018/09/10/114b76ba-af10-11e8-a20b-5f4f84429666_story.html).

16 Pew (2010) *The impact of the 2008 economic collapse*, 28 April (www.pewtrusts.org/en/research-and-analysis/reports/2010/04/28/the-impact-of-the-september-2008-economic-collapse).

17 See https://esrc.ukri.org/public-engagement/social-science-for-schools/resources/the-global-financial-crisis

18 Danny Dorling (2016) 'Brexit: The decision of a divided country', *BMJ*, 354, i3697 (www.bmj.com/content/354/bmj.i3697).

19 Shabi (2019) 'How immigration became Britain's most toxic political issue'.

20 www.youtube.com/watch?v=IldMnsymDo0

21 Home Office (2020) 'Hate crime, England and Wales, 2019/20' (www.gov.uk/government/statistics/hate-crime-england-and-wales-2019-to-2020/hate-crime-england-and-wales-2019-to-2020).

22 See https://appgbritishmuslims.org/publications

23 The Muslim Council of Britain (2021) 'Defining Islamophobia: Comprehensive report amplifies what it is, what it isn't and why it matters', 3 March (https://mcb.org.uk/press-releases/defining-islamophobia-comprehensive-report-amplifies-what-it-is-what-it-isnt-and-why-it-matters).

24 Trevor Phillips (2019) 'The notion of "Islamophobia" is being used to stifle honest debate', *The Spectator*, 7 September (www.spectator.co.uk/article/the-notion-of-islamophobia-is-being-used-to-stifle-honest-debate).

25 Phillips (2019) 'The notion of "Islamophobia"'.

26 Melanie Phillips (2018) 'Islamophobia is a fiction to shut down debate', *The Times*, 7 May (www.thetimes.co.uk/article/islamophobia-is-a-fiction-to-shut-down-debate-wwtzggnc7).

27 Leonie B. Jackson (2017) *Islamophobia in Britain: The making of a Muslim enemy*, Cham: Springer Nature.

28 Milly Williamson and Gholam Khiabany (2010) 'UK: The veil and the politics of racism', *Race & Class*, 52(2), 85–96 (https://journals.sagepub.com/doi/abs/10.1177/0306396810377003).

29 Adam Bienkov (2020) 'Boris Johnson called gay men "tank-topped bumboys" and black people "piccaninnies" with "watermelon smiles"', *Business Insider*, 9 June (www.businessinsider.com/boris-johnson-record-sexist-homophobic-and-racist-comments-bumboys-piccaninnies-2019-6?r=US&IR=T).

30 Bienkov (2020) 'Boris Johnson'.

31 See http://archive.spectator.co.uk/article/16th-july-2005/12/just-dont-call-it-war

32 Tahir Abbas (2020) 'Islamophobia as racialised biopolitics in the United Kingdom', *Philosophy & Social Criticism*, 46(5), 497–511.

33 Abbas (2020) 'Islamophobia'.

Chapter 6

1 See www.parliament.uk/about/living-heritage/evolutionofparliament/houseofcommons/reformacts/overview/reformact1832

2 Kent Online (2017) 'Half of voters took bribes in Deal and Sandwich election scandal', 5 June (www.kentonline.co.uk/sandwich/news/election-tainted-by-widespread-bribery-126738).

Notes

3   https://youtu.be/NhXYGlQOT9I

4   https://uk.gofundme.com/f/Topple-Boris

5   See www.statista.com/statistics/257337/total-lobbying-spending-in-the-us

6   Kaitlin Washburn (2018) 'What Trump's major donors are spending in the midterms', OpenSecrets, 30 October (www.opensecrets.org/news/2018/10/what-trumps-major-donors-are-spending-in-the-midterms).

7   Peter Geoghegan (2020) *Democracy for sale: Dark money and dirty politics*, London: Head of Zeus Ltd, p 3.

8   Geoghegan (2020) *Democracy for sale*, p 3.

9   www.ft.com/content/4362e62f-00fc-4cd9-a20b-9134bc2f0699

10 BBC News (2020) 'Greensill: What is the David Cameron lobbying row about?', 9 August (www.bbc.co.uk/news/uk-politics-56578838).

11 Heather Stewart and Kalyeena Makortoff (2021) 'Business card puts Greensill founder at the heart of Downing Street', *The Guardian*, 30 March (www.theguardian.com/politics/2021/mar/30/business-card-puts-greensill-founder-at-the-heart-of-downing-street).

12 BBC News (2020) 'Greensill'.

13 BBC News (2020) 'Greensill'.

14 Transparency International UK (2015) 'For lobbying in the UK, it's time for a change', 13 October (www.transparency.org.uk/lobbying-uk-its-time-change).

15 House of Commons Political and Constitutional Reform Committee (2013) *The government's lobbying bill, Seventh Report of Session 2013–14*, London: The Stationery Office Ltd (https://publications.parliament.uk/pa/cm201314/cmselect/cmpolcon/601/601.pdf).

16 Transparency International UK (2021) 'Concern over corruption red flags in 20% of UK's PPE procurement', Press Release, 21 April (www.transparency.org.uk/track-and-trace-uk-PPE-procurement-corruption-risk-VIP-lane).

17 *The BMJ* (2021) 'Covid-19: One in five government contracts had signs of possible corruption, report finds', 373, 1072 (www.bmj.com/content/373/bmj.n1072/related).

18 David Pegg (2021) 'Fifth of UK Covid contracts "raised red flags for possible corruption"', *The Guardian*, 22 April (www.theguardian.com/world/2021/apr/22/fifth-of-uk-covid-contracts-raised-red-flags-for-possible-corruption).

19 Jack Peat (2021) 'Pub landlord celebrated lucrative Covid contract by buying £1.3m country manor', *The London Economic*, 7 May (www.thelondoneconomic.com/news/pub-landlord-celebrated-lucrative-covid-contract-by-buying-1-3m-country-manor-279915).

20 Transparency International UK (2021) *Track and trace*, April (www.transparency.org.uk/track-and-trace-uk-PPE-procurement-corruption-risk-VIP-lane-research).

21 BBC News (2018) 'Johnson: £160k tennis match did take place', 18 March (www.bbc.co.uk/news/uk-politics-43448559).

22 Committee on Standards in Public Life (2011) 'Political party finance: Ending the big donor culture', Press notice, 22 November (https:// assets.publishing.service.gov.uk/government/uploads/system/uploads/ attachment_data/file/338057/20111122_Political_party_finance_ending_ big_donor_culture.pdf).

23 Oliver Heath (2015) 'Has the rise of middle class politicians led to the decline of class voting in Britain?', LSE Blog, 12 February (https://blogs. lse.ac.uk/politicsandpolicy/the-rise-of-middle-class-politicians-and-the- decline-of-class-voting-in-britain).

24 Oliver Heath (2013) 'Policy representation, social representation and class voting in Britain', *British Journal of Political Science*, 45(1), 173–93 (www.cambridge.org/core/journals/british-journal-of-political-science/ article/abs/policy-representation-social-representation-and-class-voting- in-britain/B4D4CF4C70C84BB07F4D36C5A13FAB7A).

25 Heath (2015) 'Has the rise of middle class politicians ...'.

26 Luke Audickas and Richard Cracknell (2020) *Social background of MPs 1979–2019*, Briefing Paper Number CBP 7483, 27 March, London: House of Commons Library (https://researchbriefings.files.parliament. uk/documents/CBP-7483/CBP-7483.pdf).

27 Ed Jones (2017) 'These figures show how out-of-touch UK politicians are from everyone else', Open Democracy, 2 June (www.opendemocracy. net/en/opendemocracyuk/these-figures-show-how-out-of-touch-uk- politicians-are-from-everyone-else).

28 Institute for Government (2020) 'Public funding for political parties', 26 February (www.instituteforgovernment.org.uk/explainers/public- funding-political-parties).

29 Anne Applebaum (2019) 'The more we learn about Brexit, the more crooked it looks', *The Washington Post*, March.

Chapter 7

1 *The BMJ* (2021) 'Covid-19: G7 vaccine fails to meet scale of challenge, says critics', 373, 1520 (www.bmj.com/content/373/bmj.n1520).

2 Aleem Maqbool (2020) 'Black Lives Matter: From social media post to global movement', BBC News, 10 July (www.bbc.co.uk/news/world-us- canada-53273381).

3 Matthew Taylor, Jonathan Watts and John Bartlett (2019) 'Climate crisis: 6 million people join latest wave of global protests', *The Guardian*, 27 September (www.theguardian.com/environment/2019/sep/27/ climate-crisis-6-million-people-join-latest-wave-of-worldwide-protests).

4 Somini Sengupta (2019) 'Protesting climate change, young people take to streets in a global strike', *The New York Times*, 20 September (www. nytimes.com/2019/09/20/climate/global-climate-strike.html).

5 Sharif Mustajib (2017) 'The contemporary debate on political globalization and nation-state', Voice of International Affairs, 20 July (https:// internationalaffairsbd.com/political-globalization-nation-state).

6 Mustajib (2017) 'The contemporary debate', p 68.

7   Chloe Chaplain (2019) 'General Election 2019 timetable: The key dates and deadlines for the next five weeks of campaigning', *i*, 4 November (https://inews.co.uk/news/politics/general-election-2019-timetable-deadline-voting-results-824989).

Chapter 8

1   Bart Cammaerts (2016) 'Our report found that 75% of press coverage misrepresents Jeremy Corbyn – we can't ignore media bias anymore', *Independent*, 19 July (www.independent.co.uk/voices/jeremy-corbyn-media-bias-labour-mainstream-press-lse-study-misrepresentation-we-can-t-ignore-bias-a7144381.html).

2   Media@LSE (2016) *Journalistic representations of Jeremy Corbyn in the British press: From watchdog to attackdog*, London: London School of Economics and Political Science (www.lse.ac.uk/media-and-communications/assets/documents/research/projects/corbyn/Cobyn-Report.pdf).

3   Media@LSE (2016) *Journalistic representations of Jeremy Corbyn.*

4   Media@LSE (2016) *Journalistic representations of Jeremy Corbyn.*

5   https://twitter.com/LBC/status/850093780149702657

6   https://twitter.com/jrc1921/status/1444749517967007755

7   Matthew Weaver (2017) 'Jeremy Corbyn treated unfairly by press, says David Dimbleby', *The Guardian*, 30 May (www.theguardian.com/media/2017/may/30/jeremy-corbyn-david-dimbleby-rightwing-bias-british-newspapers).

8   www.electoralcalculus.co.uk/electdata_2010.txt

9   www.fifedirect.org.uk/topics/index.cfm?fuseaction=page.display&p2sid=10CC3530-AA3B-9CCD-63F538B9ABCE0DB5&themeid=2B892409-722D-4F61-B1CC-7DE81CC06A90

Index